The Tech Worker's Guide to Unions

Janneke Parrish

Contents

To Saskia
May your journey be changed

Introduction

Your voice has power.

This is a small statement, just a few words, but they're the words that undergird everything in this book. It's the framework every democratic society is ostensibly built on, this concept of every person sharing equally in power, but it's a framework that, within the tech industry, has been cast aside.

It needs to be repeated, though. Over and over again, for every tech worker—your voice has power.

Your voice has the power to change your company. Your voice has the power to reshape your industry. Your voice has the power to change the laws around labor. Never underestimate what the power of your voice can do.

Yet somehow, the power of our voices and the reality that this is how we shape the world around us gets lost. For many, the consequences of speaking up have ensured they do it rarely. Those who speak up against injustice in their workplace can face retaliation, diminished career prospects, or losing their jobs entirely. The consequences of speaking up can be a harsh deterrent to remembering how powerful our voices are.

When so many disincentives to speaking up and making our voices heard exist, why should we speak? Why take the risk of being blacklisted from an industry, or of being made a pariah in a job we love? We need security, and by the nature of the system we're in, speaking removes that sense of security and replaces it with scrutiny and uncertainty.

In mid-2021, a few workers at the technology giant Apple began to ask questions about pay equity, and discrimination and harassment throughout the company. Each approached the question of equity through the lens of their own experiences, initially believing they were alone in being paid less than their male colleagues, or having been retaliated against for speaking to human resources. In speaking with one another, though, these workers came to understand that their experiences were not isolated incidents, but rather, repeated, time and time again, across every level of the company and every line of business.

It was through speaking that they came to understand they weren't alone, and it was through their voices that they came to take action.

The Apple workers collected hundreds of stories, reflecting hundreds of voices, all speaking the same truth—the company wasn't treating its workers equitably. A movement coalesced around these voices, asking questions about pay equity, the company's treatment of those facing a toxic workplace, and to what extent their voices should shape the company they loved.

On March 4 2022, the company's shareholders voted by a slim margin to hold a civil rights audit, examining pay equity, discrimination, and concealment clauses. It was a historic moment, one not expected to occur, and one which would not have occurred if workers hadn't spoken up, and continued speaking, even when a multi-trillion dollar company threw its weight behind efforts to silence them.

Apple's leadership knew the secret. Voices have power. Our voices have power. Our stories, our experiences, they are the most powerful things in the world, and with them, we can topple giants.

The Apple workers succeeded not only because they spoke, but because they spoke in unison. They worked together to ensure that, even when one voice fell silent, or one story got lost, the whole of them could speak loud enough to fill the gap. One voice is powerful, but many speaking together and standing for one another are more powerful still.

This is a union.

Unions are not a new concept. As long as there have people working in a trade together, there has been some form of a union. Unions have formed the bedrock of American industry for decades, providing workers with a sense of security and knowledge that those around them would be there for them, whatever happened. Unions give power to workers and amplify their voices.

This is also why their power and ability to form has been eroded for decades to the point where, in some industries, they are unheard of. As those in power realized the check on their power that unions presented, they passed laws to mitigate or ban unions entirely. States removed worker protections, or failed to pass them in the first place. It is only when we speak that we can start to undo some of the damage that's been done.

In the wake of the COVID-19 pandemic, the same story has been repeated over and over, across every industry. Workers from every strata of society have caught a glimpse behind the curtain and gained an understanding, both of how they and their value as a human being is viewed, and how much power they hold. Stores and restaurants have been brought to a halt as workers, working through the pandemic in dangerous and underpaid conditions, have turned their backs on industries that do not value them, or have chosen to unionize to bring about change. Every day, a new Starbucks unionizes, even in the face of crippling union busting. Amazon warehouses are voting to unionize. People's voices are speaking together, and saying their well-being and their value are worth more than they are currently receiving.

The tech industry is no different. We've gotten a glimpse behind the curtain, and seen that we can have a safer and more equitable working environment, and we can be paid what we're worth. When asked to give it up and return to the status quo, we're saying no. We are choosing to leave, and we are choosing to speak.

The tech industry is unionizing.

Over the course of this book, we'll explore every facet of unionizing, from inception to going public to negotiating. We'll explore union movements throughout the tech industry, both those that succeeded and those that failed, to understand how they started, what they look like, and what we can learn from them. Each company and each union is different, but there are lessons in each of them.

Above all, though, we'll explore how to speak, how to be brave in the face of a company, and how to be powerful. A union is a movement of people, and any individual person can feel overwhelmed or small. It's normal to be daunted. It's okay to be scared. The trick is to persevere, and always know that those beside you are there for you. The trick is to speak.

We are at a moment where our voices are being heard more loudly than ever. As we come out of a pandemic, we face the choice of what kind of world we want to build. We can return to what we had before, of inequity and toxicity, or we can choose to build something better, something more equitable and sustainable, and we can choose to do it together.

We can choose to unionize. Let's get started.

1.
Organizing— What's Involved?

Organizing is a tough thing to do. It takes an emotion, mental, and even physical toll. Over the course of a campaign, it's possible to lose friends, colleagues, even some of the stability that keeps each of us grounded. Organizing can be a painful slog, with heartache at every turn.

It can also be incredible and empowering, not only for you, but for everyone you meet. What we get out of organizing can reflect what we put in. There is heartache and pain, but also triumph and celebration. There are difficult moments, but also thrills and the knowledge that what you're doing is making the world a better place.

The key to being a successful organizer is to remember what you're fighting for. Your story is your own, and your reasons for wanting to make a difference in your workplace completely valid. Successful organizing, however, requires that dedication to your ideal, whatever it may be. Whether you're looking for equal pay for equal work, corporate ethics that reflect your beliefs, the ability for you and your family to stay safe, or anything in between, staying true to what you're fighting for is vital.

Stick to what you believe, and no one can stop you. Stay true to yourself, and you can accomplish great things.

What are you fighting for?

The first step in organizing, before conversation, before research, before anything else, is a simple question. What are you fighting for? What do you want to achieve?

Every organizing campaign and every union have, at their heart, some inciting event or ideal that set them on their path. For Apple workers, that ideal was the equitable treatment of all workers. Throughout their organizing, this ideal of equity and the knowledge they had of what Apple could do better remained their guiding light and kept them focused on that goal of equity.

Each union has its own goal without which it cannot succeed. To really answer the question, it's helpful to look at the context in which you're organizing, the work that's been done before, and the work that still needs to be done. With that in mind, let's break down how to establish your union's guiding light.

What should I fight for?

It's likely there's a reason you picked up this book. It's likely you understand there is something in your workplace you would like to change, but either haven't been able to change it, or don't necessarily know where to start. It doesn't even necessarily have to be that there's something wrong. Just recognizing there's something that ought to change can still be the impetus for a union.

Unions exist to help right the imbalance that exists at the heart of employment. In any kind of employment, there is an employer and a worker, someone who decides who has a job, and the one who does the job. There is an inherent power imbalance between the two parties. Since a worker relies on their employer for their income, and their income for their survival, a worker has less power than the employer. As a result, even when working conditions are bad or something needs to change, there are many reasons a worker might choose not to speak up or rock the boat. When one party relies on another party for their survival, that power imbalance sometimes makes it impossible for workers to stand up for themselves.

This is where unions come in.

Rather than being a single worker standing up alone, a union ensures that a worker has support and a collection of voices behind them. A company relies on its workers for survival, and so workers speaking and acting in unison create an atmosphere where the balance of power shifts towards something much more equal.

With that equality comes more power in the hands of workers. The issues a worker might have faced on their own and been unable to speak about can be resolved through a union. These issues include things like improved wages, better benefits, or improved corporate transparency. In the tech industry, unions advocate for the equal treatment of temporary, vendor, and contract (TVC) workers, remote or flexible work options, limited impact of layoffs, or corporate ethics that reflect the views of its workers.

Most issues can fall within the purview of what a union can organize around. The reason you picked up this book, the issue you've spotted but don't know how to solve, can be within the scope of the union you build. What causes a union takes on are the decisions of the people within it, and the people within it are you and your fellow workers.

That issue is valid, and it's as good a reason to unionize as any. Speak your truth, share your voice, and know that what drives you forward is the cornerstone of your future as an organizer.

What does the company have to do with it?

Much as the reasons for organizing vary from company to company and group to group, the form and strategies of a union vary depending on the company and your role within it. What works for a small group of a dozen workers won't work for a company of hundreds, and definitely won't work for a company of thousands or tens of thousands. The size of a company impacts how many people need to be reached to create a union, and changes the options for what types of unions are available, or what your union might look like.

Equally, understanding the corporate structures and oversight within your company gives you a window into understanding how decisions are made, who makes them, and how those decision makers might be persuaded. Though unions are groups of workers voicing their thoughts collectively, that process goes more smoothly with at least some understanding of what leadership looks like and what their primary concerns are. If leadership's concern is with public image or reputation, for instance, that creates more options for potential actions than if their concern is solely productivity.

Before diving into organizing, take a moment to understand the size and structure of your company. Are you in a small start-up, focused on receiving its next round of funding? Are you in a large multi-national with thousands of people and a CEO you've only ever seen on the news? While unions can find a home in any size or type of company, understanding the nuances of your company lays the groundwork to understand what type of union and what strategies might work best for you.

Your role within the company

Your role also has an impact. While any worker can be a union organizer, some roles are inherently more inter-connected than others. A project manager, for example, may have more cross-company connections than a call center worker by nature of each of their roles. Both are equally capable of creating unions, but the strategies they use and the connections they leverage may look different.

Consider your role and the people you interact with on a daily basis. Whether you are speaking to dozens of your fellow workers each day, or just one or two, you have the potential to build a union. It is not your role or your importance in the company that makes the difference, but the power of your conviction and what you're fighting for. Your role informs your experience, and that, in turn, informs how you speak to people, what you speak about, and who you speak to.

Use your role to your advantage, whatever it may be. No one is too big or too small to make all the difference.

What's happening here?

Each company has its own culture and its own skeletons in the closet. While every organizer has their own motivation for why they personally are organizing, that organizing happens within a context. Understanding and fitting that motivation within a greater context strengthens it and helps others see themselves in the narrative the union is crafting about a workplace and why it would benefit from organizing.

Looking back at the Apple example from the introduction, each of the original organizers had their own reason to be organizing, ranging from remote work to pay equity to limiting discrimination and harassment. However, it was when they co-ordinated with one another that they understood the greater context in which they were working and the larger impact their work could have. This greater understanding allowed them to build a union that was more inclusive of all the myriad issues workers were experiencing.

The same is true of all unions. While organizers each have their own motivations, it's in communicating that motivation with others that it's able to be clarified and strengthened. Before diving into organizing, take a moment to understand what the company looks like from perspectives other than your own, and experiences other than your own.

This exploration also provides the key building blocks that will be needed later when the true organizing and union-building begins. Rather than needing to establish from scratch who might agree with your motivation, having done this exploration instead provides a ready-made set of people whose motivations and experiences you already know and can weave into the fabric of the new union.

Preparing to be an Organizer

Being a labor organizer is expensive.

This isn't just in the financial sense, though it's worth emphasizing that there is a significant potential cost. Organizing is expensive in terms of the mental, emotional, physical, and career toll it can take on a person. On some level, this may seem obvious. Organizing does, after all, require significant labor and an investment of belief. It is never easy to emotionally invest in something so fragile, however rewarding the payoff may be. However, choosing to start a labor movement is a significant step, and one that should not be taken without understanding what it entails.

Companies target organizers. Of the dozens of organizers I spoke to for this book, nearly all have left the companies they organized within. For organizers like Clarissa Redwine, B. Pagels-Minor, and myself, this was through the companies we organized within choosing to fire us. For other organizers, like Cher Scarlett and Jessica Gonzalez, staying at the company had become untenable, and so they chose to leave. Still others, like Shannon Wait, Aerica Shimizu Banks, and myself, have left the tech industry entirely. While each person's story and motivation are different, the reality is that being under the scrutiny of a company of any size is difficult. Facing the skepticism, scorn, and sometimes harassment of peers is traumatic. The cost of organizing can be, in every sense, overwhelming.

Your experience will be unique to you. While your particular circumstances and identity may have an impact on how your experience ultimately manifests, the course of that path lies partially with you. Being aware of the risks and preparing for them breeds greater success than going in blind. Unless you take care of yourself, any movement you seek to build cannot succeed.

Preparing your narrative

It's also important to recognize that the narrative of who you are as an organizer and why you are organizing will cease to be in your control. Both to those within your company, and those outside, your individual reasons become lost behind the veil of the reasons and motivations others ascribe to you. Who you are as a person and organizer comes under scrutiny and gets warped through the lenses of all who observe you. Having control of the narrative to the greatest extent possible is critical, not only for the success of the movement, but sometimes for your own mental and emotional well-being.

Having a clear strategy of what actions are going to be taken and a rough timeline of when can help with ensuring a consistency in organizing that bucks the narrative others are crafting. Remaining consistent in messaging and taking the time to communicate with as many people as possible also helps with crafting a message. Be prepared for the elements of your organizing that others may try to turn into weapons. Once you identify the weaknesses in your message or your methods, you can inoculate against them, either by crafting the counterarguments into your pitch, or by ignoring these criticisms. Learning to ignore criticism is critical—though it is harsh to say, there will always be cruelty. Learning not to take it personally helps make a collective movement collective, rather than becoming more about any one individual leader.

The idea of crafting and controlling the narrative isn't limited to just the time period during which you intend to be organizing, nor does it stop being important if you choose to stop organizing. The consequences of being an organizer—especially a very public one—continue to exist well into the future. When considering what kind of organizer you want to be and the particular narrative you want to craft, consider not only the particulars of the company or circumstances under which you're organizing, but also what those motivations and actions will look like in a year, five years, or a decade. Actions taken as a labor organizer are not taken in a vacuum—they are part of a movement, as is anyone who chooses to be public with their activism.

Preparing financially

It is vital to be financially secure enough to organize. While illegal, organizing carries with it the very real risk of losing one's job. Though the NLRB offers a path to restitution when a company does break the law, this path can take months or even years to navigate. Instead, it's best to have a bank of savings in case a company does decide it's simpler to fire an organizer and deal with the consequences after.

Being an organizer—and being fired for organizing—also makes it more difficult to get hired in the future, especially in cases where the firing was publicized, or references evaporated alongside the job. In my case, it took over three months from when Apple fired me to when I was offered another job. In discussing with other organizers, this timeframe is on the lower end, with it potentially taking three to six months to find another job.[1] Because of this potential gap in employment, it's useful to have at least six months to a year's worth of savings before starting to organize.

For some roles in the tech industry, this amount of savings is not feasible. Organizing should not exist solely for those who can afford it, and so, alternatives exist. GoFundMes are an effective way to help generate funds for fired organizers, though this comes with the caveat that a story has to be public enough to generate interest. GoFundMes provide a way not only for an individual organizer to stay funded, but also to generate sympathy and create public support for a movement.[2]

The Solidarity Fund by Coworker also provides a potential way for organizers to gather funds, both for the actual work of organizing,

---

1. Interview with B. Pagels-Minor, 3 November 2022

2. Interview with Jessica Gonzalez, 14 October 2022

and after experiencing potential retaliation. The Solidarity Fund not only provides training and stipends to buy organizing material and non-company equipment, but can provide funds to organizers who have lost their jobs for organizing.[3] Though this is application-based, it can help make a difference financially for those who need it[4].

Preparing legally

It is also important to either have an attorney or a plan for consulting with one. While organizing is a legally protected activity, employers are not always respectful of the law, nor does the law necessarily protect against all potential retaliation. It can also be helpful to understand the legality of a particular action or how taking that action might impact any potential case. While a lawyer isn't needed to become an activist, having a plan of who to talk to, or even talking to one in advance to check what your NDA does and does not allow, as well as what local laws are applicable can be extremely helpful.

Training

In addition to preparing your immediate situation, it can also be helpful to learn more about being an organizer through formal training. While not necessary, these trainings can provide a context to learn and hone your skills before talking to anyone in your workplace. These can also provide more information about what resources are available in your area, or what your local laws look like. Most major national

---

3. https://coworkerfund.org/

4. Interview with Laurence Berland, 10 October 2022

unions provide organizer training. A list of some of these trainings has been included in the resources section of this book.

Setting your limits

Know your own limits, and recognize when to step back. Caring for yourself throughout this process is the most important thing, especially if you are organizing because of a toxic work environment, harassment, or other abuses. Organizing is a drain on mental and emotional health, and no movement succeeds when its members burn out.

One example of the importance of setting limits and creating an organization built on trust comes from B. Pagels-Minor, a former organizer at Netflix. In October 2021, Netflix began streaming the Dave Chappelle comedy special "The Closer," in which Chappelle based some of his comedy on transphobia. Workers at Netflix protested, arguing that Netflix's choice to air the special dehumanized trans workers and further flamed the fires of transphobia. In response, Netflix CEO Ted Sarandos sent out an internal memo, arguing that the special would lead to "no real world harm."[5]

For organizers like Pagels-Minor, this brushing off of their concerns was a clear sign that management was not interested in engaging in a good faith conversation.[6] Trans activists and allies within Netflix partnered with groups outside Netflix and together organized a walkout and protest against the special and in favor of Netflix taking

---

5. https://www.nbcnews.com/pop-culture/tv/more-100-people -rally-outside-netflix-protest-dave-chappelle-s-n1281994

6. Interview with B. Pagels-Minor, 3 November 2022

concrete steps to support trans creators, hire more diverse talent, and flag anti-trans content on the platform.[7] This walkout, though small, garnered international attention and generated exactly the conversation that trans employees had been looking for. The Chappelle special became a focal point for better understanding transphobia in media and what the role of streaming services like Netflix is in promoting content, as well as how said content could lead to real-world harm.

However, the protest was not without risk for the organizers. Though most of the organizers remained anonymous, two organizers—Terra Field and B. Pagels-Minor—became the focal points for journalists because of the actions Netflix took against them. Field was suspended from Netflix for attending a meeting she had not been invited to, and Pagels-Minor was fired for allegedly leaking confidential documents to the media.[8]

For Pagels-Minor, Netflix's action shifted the narrative from what they'd wanted it to be to one beyond their control. "I don't want to be the face of anything," Pagels-Minor said, but with Netflix's action, the choice, to a certain extent, was out of their hands. They and Field became the image of what happens when one chooses to stand up against a major tech company, and they became someone who, whether they wanted to be or not, was seen as a leader.[9]

---

7. https://www.theguardian.com/media/2021/oct/20/netflix-employees-activism-walkout-dave-chappelle-controversy

8. https://www.theguardian.com/media/2021/oct/20/netflix-employees-activism-walkout-dave-chappelle-controversy

9. Interview with B. Pagels-Minor, 3 November 2022

Critically, Pagels-Minor had the training and strategy to decide how to approach becoming one of the faces of the Netflix protests.[10] Pagels-Minor chose to give interviews to a limited number of publications. They wrote an op-ed in the Washington Post, leveraging the publicity surrounding the protests into a wider forum for discussing why the protest mattered and what lay at its heart. Though they did not choose to be in the forefront, because of preparation and planning, they turned that publicity into a way to further the movement they now represented.

The protests were also somewhat successful. Because of the attention brought to the protests and the hard work of the organizers, substantive changes occurred at Netflix. Netflix began to have greater transparency around terminations, creating a culture that better supported understanding why Netflix leadership was taking a particular action, and providing a better conduit for workers to discuss these actions with each other. The protests around the Dave Chappelle special also recontextualized Netflix and its influence on media. Whereas it had previously been more of an opaque goliath, the controversy around "The Closer" cultivated a climate in which Netflix could be held more accountable and could be more questioned by the media at large.[11]

However, as Pagels-Minor aptly stated, "the accolades of winning the battle are not enough." For both Pagels-Minor and Field, this attention to the protests came at the cost of their jobs, as well as the financial, emotional, and mental toll. Knowing the outcome, when asked if they would take the same actions, Pagels-Minor said "I'm not

---

10. Interview with B. Pagels-Minor, 3 November 2022

11. Interview with B. Pagels-Minor, 3 November 2022

sure I would do it again."[12] Despite the changes that the protests ushered in, the reality of the cost of organizing means that very real choices must be made about whether to bear those costs, and how far to go in an action.

Recognizing your risk

Some workers are more at risk of facing retaliation—and facing more severe retaliation—than others. Historically marginalized groups are chronically under-represented in tech, with 26.7% of tech workers being women, and 7.4% of all tech workers being Black.[13] Workers in historically marginalized groups tend to be more isolated than their cis-hetero white male counterparts, receiving fewer promotion opportunities, lower wages, and worse performance reviews.[14] In a context where some workers are already seen as lesser by virtue of who they are, companies are less hesitant to take action against an organizer.

Most of the organizers interviewed for this book are women. Most identify as LGBTQ+. Most identify as BIPOC. This is not because these categories represent the majority of organizers, but rather, because these are the organizers companies are more likely to retaliate harshly against. The reality of organizing is that it is less safe for some to be organizers than others. When deciding whether or not to become

---

12. Interview with B. Pagels-Minor, 3 November 2022

13. https://www.cnbc.com/2022/02/24/jobs-for-the-future-repo rt-highlights-need-for-tech-opportunities-for-black-talent.html

14. https://cmr.berkeley.edu/2017/08/diversity-in-tech/

an organizer, it is important not only to consider those things that are in your control, but also, those things that are not.

"Accolades of winning the battle are not enough,"[15] nor is it enough to start a movement, but lose yourself in the process. The decision to begin organizing is a big one, with potentially life-altering consequences. Every workplace benefits from a union, and organizing always helps the collective, but it is worth considering that that collective good sometimes comes at the cost of the individual. Before beginning to organize, take a moment to consider your risks. Consider if you are secure enough financially, mentally, and emotionally, and if you are prepared for what might lie ahead.

So, what are you fighting for?

A single voice has power. Voices echoing one and amplifying one another have more power. Never discount the power of one person asking a question. Any voice could be the one that starts the conversation. Any labor movement is a collection of people, their thoughts and ideas coming together to form something greater than any of them could accomplish individually. As Apple organizer Steven McGrath put it: "You can't just assume somebody else is going to take care of it. You don't know when it might be you who makes the difference."[16]

We've looked at what fuels organizing and what drives people to use their voices. We are all shaped by the circumstances around us, and what is possible for where we are. Before reading on, take a moment to consider your own workplace, its size, its structure, and where you

---

15. Interview with B. Pagels-Minor, 3 November 2022

16. Interview with Steven McGrath, 26 September 2022

fall within it. Place yourself in the narrative that you'll craft around organizing. What is it that drives you forward? What is it that you're fighting for?

Hold that idea in your mind as you continue through this book. As you build a union in your workplace, you'll face barriers, difficulties, and moments of doubt. That idea, that thing you're fighting for, that is what will see you through to the end. Stay true to what you believe, and trust in the power of your voice.

Equally, before leaping into the pool of organizing, map out your own situation and understand how the costs of organizing might impact you. Ask yourself:

- Do I have a financial safety net in case I lose my job?

- Do a have a support network to help me?

- Do I want to be known publicly, or would I prefer to stay anonymous?

- Do I have another option if I lose my job?

- Am I at greater risk than some of my peers for retaliation?

Couple these questions with more practical ones to form a more complete picture of yourself and what you are setting out to do:

- What is my goal with organizing? Do I want to build a union, or achieve something else?

- How can I tell the story of why I'm organizing?

By understanding the risks you're taking and how to mitigate them in advance, you are much better prepared as an organizer. Having a plan and charting your course ahead of time makes it easier to weather the storm ahead of you.

The fantastic thing about organizing is that there is rarely a point where an organizer decides to become an organizer. There are steps that a person takes to understand the world around them, and over the course of those steps, they realize some injustice. It is in that moment of realization that each person faces a choice. They can walk away and continue, aware of the injustice, but choosing not to act, or they could take a stand and do something about it. Organizers are those who, in the face of injustice, choose to act. You can be an organizer. All it takes is recognizing injustice, believing in the potential for change, and deciding to take a stand. You can do this. Let's understand how.

2. How the tech industry's structures discourage unionizing

We've discussed the power of using your voice to speak up about issues and injustices in your workplace. It is important to remember, though, that the very structure of the tech industry is rife with systems that keep people from speaking up. From NDAs to compensation structures, there's a lot at stake for organizers wanting to build a union in their workplace. In this section, we will look at some of the hazards of organizing. Some of these are intentional efforts by companies to keep workers from speaking out. Others are more subtle, banking on workers' own need for financial stability, or the company's desire to keep overhead low. Knowing what obstacles might lie in your path can help you better understand how to navigate them and stay focused on your goal.

Ready to go? Then let's take a look at the obstacle course ahead.

NDAs and Cultures of Secrecy

One element of organizing unique to the tech industry is the impact of non-disclosure agreements, or NDAs. While the core intention of these is to protect trade secrets in the fast-paced world of tech, in practice, the potential penalties can intimidate workers into silence and make workers reluctant to organize. Often, when beginning a unionization campaign, NDAs are one of the first obstacles an organizer needs to overcome.

Non-disclosure agreements

Non-disclosure agreements (or NDAs) are common in the tech industry. Most, if not all, workers in the tech industry have signed some variation of an NDA in one job or another, whether it's called an NDA, confidentiality agreement, or some other term.

NDAs prevent workers from discussing the specifics of their work with competitors, essentially ensuring that a worker can't be a source of information for a rival company. The extent and severity of NDAs can vary from company to company, with some only asking that specific techniques be kept confidential, while others require absolute secrecy about every element of a worker's endeavors.

However, NDAs have also come to be used for more than protecting intellectual property and trade secrets. In addition to work-related secrecy, NDAs have included implications that everything related to the workplace is meant to be kept secret, and that speaking publicly about one's experiences at a company might be grounds for a lawsuit based on breaching an NDA. The penalties for this could range from disciplinary action within the workplace, to losing one's job, to facing a lawsuit from a former employer.

Workers who sign NDAs are generally aware that there are penalties for breaking said NDA, and these penalties are a significant disincentive for most workers to unionize. While this should be the case about intellectual property, a consequence of the fear of penalties is not speaking about workplace conditions or abuse in the workplace.

NDAs, as a consequence of the fear they cause, can be used to suppress workers' voices.

Cultures of Secrecy

Beyond NDAs, many companies may also have a culture of secrecy. As an example, one reason Apple workers in the introduction were not aware of the issues their colleagues faced was because of the company's culture of secrecy. Where Apple worked to ensure its workers understood their work was highly confidential, an additional consequence was that workers believed discussing their work in any capacity was grounds for termination.

Fostering a culture of secrecy also creates a culture that can self-enforce and ostracize those that are perceived to be violating the company's trust, even if they are not actually doing so. To go to our Apple example again, one experience shared by several of the AppleTogether organizers was that of being looked at with greater scrutiny by their peers, or accused of leaking proprietary information when they had not done so. For some, the act of speaking out at all, regardless of the legality of doing so, is a betrayal of the spirit of an NDA or a violation of company culture. Especially for those who care deeply about the company they work for or the work they do, this idea that speaking is a betrayal can be daunting, and can prevent people from organizing.

The impact of secrecy and NDAs on organizing

This combination of contracts ensuring workers do not share proprietary information or leak trade secrets with cultures of secrecy and siloing can be effective barriers to organizing. After all, if a potential consequence of speaking to someone about thoughts and experiences can be grounds for termination, the risks are higher than many can accept.

Before speaking out about workplace issues, it is critical to understand what an NDA does and does not cover:

- NDAs cover proprietary information, such as how a product or process works. They generally apply both while working for a company and once that employment ends.

- They cannot, however, cover discussion of working conditions or wages, or prohibit you from speaking with regulatory bodies or the media.

- Your right to speak about your work experience is protected.

However, for some workers, especially those working within a culture of secrecy, knowing these rights is not enough to overcome the cultural pressure to not discuss working conditions or wages. In these cases, it's helpful to remind people of their rights and to provide more detailed information about what rights are protected by state and federal law. Setting the example can also be helpful. By speaking first, you set the stage by showing you're both aware of your rights and unafraid to break a culture of silence. Sharing your working conditions or salary with a worker who is worried speaking might violate their NDA sets

the example that this speech is protected, and that they are not alone
in speaking.

Do your homework

Before speaking to others – either inside or outside your company -
about your workplace experiences, review your NDA and make sure
you're aware of what it does and does not cover. While we will explore
your rights in more detail in a later chapter, a good rule of thumb
is that an NDA cannot legally forbid you from discussing workplace
conditions, regardless of which state you live in. This means you are
free to discuss wages and compensation, safety and safety issues (including discrimination), and workplace conditions.[1] When communicating with your colleagues internally, these topics are considered
protected, and discussing them is not a violation of an NDA.

When discussing these issues outside the workplace, however, it's
important to keep in mind the limitations on what constitutes workplace conditions. Again, while this generally includes wages, compensation, safety issues, and general conditions, signing some types of
NDAs may preclude discussing some aspects of this. If you have signed
a non-disparagement agreement, that agreement may limit your free-
dom of speech. Most standard NDAs will not be able to limit your
ability to speak about working conditions, but it is important to be
aware if you are in that rare minority.

While speaking about working conditions is protected speech,
naming specific people or unverifiable experiences may not be. Dis-

---

1. https://www.nlrb.gov/about-nlrb/rights-we-protect/your-rig
   hts/employee-rights

cussing ethical concerns regarding unreleased products may also not be protected speech. A good rule of thumb is that what you want to say should not be directed at an individual, and should not share information regarding unreleased products, products' inner-workings, or other proprietary information. You can talk about how you work and what it's like to do your work, but not what you're working on or how it works.

If you are considering speaking publicly and have signed an NDA, it is wise to speak with an attorney about what your NDA does and does not cover before going forward. Depending on what you want to say, whistleblower protection laws and organizations may be able to provide more assistance as well.

How to work around NDAs

While NDAs can't exactly be worked around, the culture of fear and secrecy they create can be mitigated. Cultures of secrecy and fear spread when people don't know what their NDAs do and do not cover, or when they aren't aware of their rights.

- Providing more information to someone worried about their NDA can help give them the knowledge and confidence to recognize that an NDA can't prevent them from speaking about their working conditions or experiences with those around them.

- If you do consult an attorney to understand your NDA, you can share what the attorney told you about what your NDA does and does not cover.

- You can also share relevant laws that let others know their rights are protected.

NDAs can seem scary, and they can provide both internal and external disincentives to organizing. However, your voice and your right to discuss your working conditions are protected, more and more every day. An NDA can't stop you from organizing. If someone tells you that you can't talk to them about unions or working conditions because of an NDA, let them know that no company can silence your right to organize.

The Golden Handcuffs

There are many reasons why people choose to enter the tech industry, but generally, compensation is high on the list. The tech industry is known for its high salaries, office perks, and compensation packages, especially for engineers and highly specialized skillsets. However, these lucrative salaries and bonus structures have their downsides, leading to the term "golden handcuffs."

Broadly speaking, the term "golden handcuffs" is the idea that, as a worker's value to their employer grows, their compensation grows, increasing to the point that no other company could match their current compensation and bonuses sufficiently to make it financially viable for that worker to move to a different company. This compensation can take the form of stocks that require a minimum employment duration before they vest, bonuses that have to be paid back if a worker leaves within a certain amount of time, or other forms of special compensation that incentivize a worker to stay at a particular company. This high compensation often comes with the sense that the compensation should be earned. While that in and of itself is not a particularly radical idea, earning the high compensation often takes the form of diminishing work-life balance, working long hours or on weekends, and prioritizing work needs over other commitments, such as family. While everyone's experience with work culture and compensation packages is unique, many in the tech industry will have experienced some variation of the golden handcuffs, either through culture, or financial incentives that are hard to walk away from.

How do the golden handcuffs impact organizing?

Having one's financial future tied to a particular employer makes it difficult or scary to organize. Risking tens if not hundreds of thousands of dollars and financial stability is a daunting ask, and not an easy decision to make.

There are no reassurances about what is and is not safe to risk. While an employer cannot take away money they have already given, incentives, unvested stock, and other financial benefits disappear if an employer chooses to no longer employ a particular worker. Though not their primary purpose, golden handcuffs are a powerful systemic disincentive for workers because of how much impact they actually have.

How to work around the golden handcuffs

There is no easy answer for how to organize around the culture created by compensation packages. For some, risking their financial future is – understandably – too great a risk to take.

However, it can be helpful to put these compensation packages in context. Most workers in the tech industry do not earn large compensation packages. Sharing salary information and discussing compensation openly helps shed light on these inequities. For some, seeing that inequity can stir them to action when they otherwise might not have been willing to.

For those who are still not willing to risk their jobs, taking smaller actions can be a way to support a unionization effort without putting themselves at risk. Being a participant in a unionizing campaign rather than being an organizer is almost always a safer choice. Receiving support is still valuable, and every participant is important.

There are also legal avenues to recover lost income or compensation, or demand reinstatement, in the case of an illegal termination. The National Labor Relations Board maintains a process by which workers can file complaints if they believe their rights have been violated. There are also a wealth of private employment law firms who can advise on what to do, or who can represent you if you do face issues. Meeting with them for a free consultation can give you a better understanding of your rights and options.

Most importantly, each worker assesses their own risk level. There are some workers for whom the risks are too great. This is completely okay. Though it can be disappointing for a potential ally to decide there is too much risk involved for them to feel comfortable joining an organizing campaign, their decision must always be respected. Much as organizers' voices matter, so too do the voices of those establishing their limits. Everyone has a right to decide their own limits, and to have that decision respected.

The incentives a company offers to its workers can be powerful disincentives to organizing, but equally, workers speaking in force can cause these incentives to change from what isn't working to what is. Golden handcuffs shackle workers to employers, but employers to workers as well. Companies afraid to lose workers will listen to what they have to say. That truth places power in the hands of workers.

While no decision about finances should be made recklessly, and only you can decide for yourself what level of risk you are willing to take, golden handcuffs are a signal of indispensability. That reliance on a given worker or workers can work to your advantage. Use your voice as a group, and it gives each person more power and more safety than they would have as an individual.

H-1B Visas

While every worker has the same protections under labor law, the reality remains that companies will sometimes break the law. The consequences of companies illegally retaliating against organizers can be more dire than for others. One particular group of workers who are both particularly common and particularly vulnerable are H-1B visa holders.

Some workers who are not United States citizens or permanent residents are able to work in the United States through an H-1B visa. This type of visa is tied to employment specifically. For workers on this type of visa, they must remain employed, or, if they lose their job, find new employment within 60 days or risk deportation.[2] Workers with this visa represent approximately 13% of tech industry workers.[3]

How is organizing different for H-1B workers?

While all workers face threats to their livelihood when organizing, for H-1B workers, these threats can verge on existential. The threat of

---

2.

   https://www.forbes.com/sites/stuartanderson/2022/11/04/twitter-and-other-tech-layoffs-raise-h-1b-visa-employment-issues/

3. https://www.teamblind.com/blog/index.php/2018/08/10/h-1b-in-the-tech-industry/

deportation and the uprooting of their and their families' lives is a powerful disincentive to organizing. H-1B workers are more than able to join and be represented by a union, and are as legally protected when organizing as any other worker. However, the consequences for an H-1B worker can be much more dramatic.

In practice, this means that, while H-1B workers are more than welcome to organize their workplaces, if they are retaliated against through termination, it can be extraordinarily difficult for them to be able to maintain their visa status and find a new employer within the set time limit.

H-1B workers and organizing

In many ways, H-1B workers are some of the greatest beneficiaries of unions. Unions provide protection during layoffs, and often provide representation or guidance when workers' jobs are at risk. For those with this visa, the protection offered by a union can spell the difference between being able to stay in their homes, or being completely uprooted.

However, much like with the golden handcuffs, the risks are for each individual person to assess for themselves. H-1B workers who choose to organize risk not only their jobs, but their lives in the United States. It is completely reasonable and understandable for these workers to decide the risk is not worth it, and instead either take supporting roles, or not participate. Much like with the golden handcuffs, the decision of how and to what extent to participate is each person's own decision, and that decision must be respected.

This doesn't mean you should assume someone with an H-1B visa is not interested in organizing. The decision is, once again, each person's own. Don't assume one way or the other how a person feels about risk. Instead, provide an inclusive and welcoming space, for those who choose to participate, and the voices of those who cannot.

Temporary, Vendor, and Contract Workers

There is a growing trend of labor being done by workers who are not employees of the company they are working for. These workers are known as temporary, vendor, or contract (TVC) workers. As of 2018, roughly 20% of the American labor market was comprised of some version of TVC workers, with that number expected to be near 50% by 2030.[4] Within the tech industry, some companies' workforces can be more than half TVC workers.[5] This is especially true of large tech companies, such as Google, Meta, and Apple, where specialized work is done by contractors and gig workers for a fraction of the cost of hiring a full-time employee.

Most of these contract workers do not receive the same benefits, compensation, or even treatment as their full-time peers, even when potentially sharing the same workspace. These workers may be denied participation in social functions or benefits, or even have diminished protections in place to ensure their health and safety. At companies that use a large number of contract workers, this differential treatment creates a hierarchy between full-time and contract workers that can be hard for contract workers to reconcile.

---

4. https://www.npr.org/2018/01/22/578825135/rise-of-the-contract-workers-work-is-different-now

5. https://www.nytimes.com/2019/05/28/technology/google-temp-workers.html

The experience of contract workers varies dramatically, depending on the country they work in, the company they contract for, or even the particular department. For some, the experience can be deeply siloed, with no sense that work is done for a larger company, other than language on a contract.[6] For others, they might work alongside full-time employees, doing the same work and reporting to the same supervisors, but for significantly less money than their full-time counterparts.[7]

TVC Workers and Unions

It's important to make a decision about whether or not to include TVC workers in your unionizing campaign. To make that decision, it's important to understand what it is to be a contract worker at a large company, and what union representation can mean.

On the face of it, it may seem like a workers' union can make a difference for contracted workers, and indeed, should do so. Unions fundamentally focus on the collective well-being of workers, and contracted workers, even if they share a different employer, can be seen as falling under that umbrella of collective well-being.

However, the experience and circumstances under which a contract worker works can have a dramatic impact on whether or not they see themselves as part of the ecosystem of a larger company. Whether or not a worker sees themselves as part of a greater corporate ecosystem

---

6. Interview with Robert Howell, 15 October 2022

7. Interview with an anonymous Malaysian contract worker, 14 October 2022

informs whether or not they welcome being represented by a larger union.

When building a union, it is imperative to consider whether or not you will include TVC workers in your union. They are workers within your company's ecosystem, but may have a wholly different experience, or may not believe a union of the overall company can understand or represent their interests.

TVC workers are also at greater risk for retaliation, both by the larger company and their specific employer, as their organizing could be seen as putting their employer's contract with the larger company at risk. Much like with H-1B workers, TVC workers have unique vulnerabilities that must be considered.

Incorporating TVC workers

As with all groups we've discussed, the best way to understand whether or not TVC workers should be included in your union is through conversation. Engaging with your fellow workers – and seeing them as fellow workers – grants a perspective that you might not otherwise have, and can clarify whether your fellow workers would prefer to have their own union or be represented by yours.

Legally, TVC workers may or may not be able to represented in a contract union; however, it's important to have the conversation and determine whether or not TVC workers will be included before examining the legal elements. Even if the particular arrangement in your company does not allow for TVC workers to be included, establishing that they do want representation allows the union to advocate on their behalf, even if they are not formal members.

The siloing and separation of labor between full-time and contracted workers means there are gaps to be bridged in any corporate structure. Though all workers within the same ecosystem, in some cases, the barriers created by a contract can be ones contracted workers would prefer to maintain, while others prefer to see them fall. Ultimately, the decision of how to engage with contracted workers is one that must be made by each union, but always with compassion and empathy.

I can overcome these barriers!

Unionizing is difficult under any circumstances, but the structure of the tech industry provides unique difficulties to organizing that should be considered and strategized around.

Before beginning your organizing campaign, look at your company's structure to determine which of the structural disincentives we've discussed apply. If you work for a large company, all of them are likely in place, while a smaller company may only have a few.

Remember:

- Counter NDAs with knowledge of your rights, confirming your rights with an attorney, and sharing your knowledge.

- Counter the golden handcuffs by discussing salaries and benefits openly, participating without directly organizing, and recognizing that highly paid employees are also valuable to the company.

- Counter the inequality of H-1B visas by being open and empathetic to workers who choose not to organize directly.

- Counter the inequality of TVC workers by deciding whether to include TVC workers and including their viewpoints if they choose to be represented by the union

3. Rights Make Might

Companies hold a lot of power, but so do you. Whether it be through withholding your labor, speaking out, or just having conversations with your fellow workers, you hold a lot of power to change your workplace for the better.

More importantly, many of the most common ways in which you express that power are protected by law. Decades of work by labor activists like you has ensured that your ability to organize and unionize is protected, at least to a point.

We will explore how to ensure your rights are safeguarded, and what to do when you believe they have been violated. While it is important to keep in mind that laws vary from country to country, state to state, and even sometimes from city to city, there are some broad, overarching protections that we will explore.

Above all else, though, this section is an affirmation of your abilities. This section is about you, how much weight stands behind you, and the power you never knew you had. If anything you've read so far has been discouraging, let this be the encouragement. You have rights. You have power.

Let's dive in.

The National Labor Relations Act and the National Labor Relations Board

The core federal law that governs unions is the National Labor Relations Act, or NLRA. It was passed in 1935 as part of a slew of other acts designed to grant more power to workers and help rectify the inequality that plagued America. The NLRA ensured that workers had the right to act and bargain collectively with their employers. Though the NLRA has changed over time, its fundamental principles—that workers have the right to collectively discuss and act with each other—hold firm.

The NLRA guarantees that workers have the right to discuss wages, working conditions, and benefits. They are welcome to do so off company property and off company time and equipment, though activities like circulating petitions, wearing solidarity clothing or pins, raising questions or objections in company meetings, or staging walkouts or strikes are also protected. Workers also have the right to discuss their working conditions with the public on social media, or speak with journalists. Workers also have every right to speak with government agencies, law enforcement, or lawyers. Crucially for unionization efforts, employers cannot interfere with unionization efforts by threatening, making promises, holding captive audience meetings, or asking individual workers about their union sympathies. Worker protections are broad, and no NDA can preclude any of the above rights.[1]

There are a lot of terms at play here, though. To understand what "collective bargaining" and "collective action" actually mean, it's helpful to look at the text of the NLRA. It's first important to note who is protected by it, as not all workers are.

Who is a worker?

The NLRA specifically protects the rights of "employees," whom it defines as:

The term "employee" shall include any employee, and shall not be limited to the employees of a particular employer, unless the Act [this subchapter] explicitly states otherwise, and shall include any individual whose work has ceased as a consequence of, or in connection with, any current labor dispute or because of any unfair labor practice, and who has not obtained any other regular and substantially equivalent employment, but shall not include any individual employed as an agricultural laborer, or in the domestic service of any family or person at his home, or any individual employed by his parent or spouse, or any individual having the status of an independent contractor, or any individual employed as a supervisor, or any individual employed by an employer subject to the Railway Labor Act [45 U.S.C. § 151 et seq.], as amended from time to time, or by any other person who is not an employer as herein defined.

1.

https://www.employer.gov/EmploymentIssues/Union-and-pro
tected-concerted-activity/What-are-my-employees-rights-under
-the-NLRA/

In plain terms, a person who does work for a company, but is not an independent contractor, supervisor, or some other temporary worker qualifies as an employee and is protected by the NLRA.

Who is a supervisor?

For our purposes, it's important to also understand who qualifies as an "independent contractor" and "supervisor." The NLRA provides an answer to the latter:

The term "supervisor" means any individual having authority, in the interest of the employer, to hire, transfer, suspend, lay off, recall, promote, discharge, assign, reward, or discipline other employees, or responsibly to direct them, or to adjust their grievances, or effectively to recommend such action, if in connection with the foregoing the exercise of such authority is not of a merely routine or clerical nature, but requires the use of independent judgment.

A supervisor is anyone with power over the employment status of employees, or with the capability of making independent decisions over what work is done by whom. This means that anyone for whom assigning and monitoring work to others and ultimately being responsible for the outcome of that work is a supervisor.[2] Supervisors are not protected by the NLRA. Though they may be subject to adverse working conditions that may lead them to want to join a union, they are unable to do so, and can get fired for advocating others form a union. If you are a supervisor, while you are certainly welcome to read

---

2. https://katten.com/files/20780_Labor_Board_Clarifies_Defini
tion_of_Supervisors_Unable_To_Unionize.pdf

the rest of this chapter, please keep in mind that much of it will not apply to you.

Temporary, Vendor, and Contract Workers

The one other important element of the NLRA's coverage that is particularly important in the context of tech organizing is independent contractors. As previously discussed, an increasingly large percentage of the work done in the tech industry is done by contractors, though the line of who qualifies as an contractor may be hazy. It is, however, extremely important to know which side of the line a worker falls on. Employees are protected by the NLRA; contractors may or may not be.

The NLRB uses a concept known as "joint employer" in cases where a person is employed by one company, but who is also doing work for another.[3] As of this writing, the NLRB's rule for joint employment is:

an employer is a joint employer of particular employees if the employer has an employment relationship with those employees under established common-law agency principles and the employer shares or codetermines those matters governing at least one of the employees' essential terms and conditions of employment

In plain terms, if a worker's work is directed by a company other than the one they are directly employed by, the company is a joint employer. This means that both the direct employer and the larger company are responsible if there is illegal retaliation against a worker.

---

3. https://www.federalregister.gov/documents/2022/09/07/2022 -19181/standard-for-determining-joint-employer-status

One example of joint employment can be found with Shannon Wait, and her experience within the Alphabet ecosystem. In February 2021, Shannon Wait worked for the Google data center services subcontractor Modis. Though not a direct Google employee, Wait was a member of the Alphabet Workers Union (AWU-CWA), and considered herself part of the Google ecosystem.[4]

In response to issues around pay and access to water, Wait began encouraging her colleagues to discuss their pay and bonuses, and speaking publicly about her concerns about the discrepancy in working conditions and pay between her and full-time Alphabet employees. Despite these discussions being protected speech, Wait was suspended for her organizing and public support of AWU-CWA.[5]

The firing of Shannon Wait provided an opportunity for the newly formed AWU-CWA to show its ability to make a difference in the lives of workers, not only on a collective level, but on an individual level as well. Shannon Wait's status as a contracted worker also provided an opportunity to show how a union could embrace all workers within a company's ecosystem, not just those who explicitly worked for the large company.

AWU-CWA filed two charges with the National Labor Relations Board (NLRB) on Wait's behalf. The first alleged that Wait had been illegally suspended for discussing working conditions. The second alleged that Modis had illegally suppressed her ability to discuss her wages. In March 2021, AWU-CWA and Wait won. Wait's suspension

---

4. Interview with Shannon Wait, 8 December 2022

5. https://www.datacenterdynamics.com/en/news/alphabet-work ers-union-files-labor-complaint-against-google-data-center-cont ractor/

was overturned, and Google and Modis reaffirmed workers' rights to discuss pay and working conditions.[6]

Though Wait was not a direct employee of Google, because Google directed her work, Google was seen as a co-employer. This meant that her case not only impacted her direct employer, but Google as well, and her impact stretched well beyond the walls of the data center in which she worked.

In addition, it's possible for a worker to be misclassified as a temporary, vendor, or contract worker, depriving them not only of the compensation they ought to be receiving, but also of their legal rights. One famous example is in the case of *Vizcaino v. Microsoft*, a case which resulted in companies throughout the tech industry ensuring their documentation contained explicit instructions on who did and did not qualify as an independent contractor. In *Vizcaino*, workers working at Microsoft signed documents defining them as independent contractors, but were in almost every way, treated as employees rather than contractors. They did the same work as employees, worked in the same area as employees, had e-mail addresses that didn't mark them as non-employees, reported to managers at Microsoft, and in every way, seemed identical to the employees around them. However, Microsoft did not offer them the same benefits it offered employees, such as healthcare and a 401k. After an investigation by the IRS, these workers were found to be employees, not contractors. Vizcaino and seven other workers filed suit against Microsoft, asking for financial compensation equivalent to the benefits they had not received due

---

6. https://www.bbc.com/news/technology-56659212

to being misclassified as contractors rather than employees. In 1997, Vizcaino and the other workers won their case.[7]

Though this case is from the late 90s, the implications of it still ring throughout the tech industry, and the questions it raises are still valid. Even within the NLRB, the definition of "independent contractor" is in flux and unclear. Recent decisions around Uber drivers and FedEx delivery persons highlight how the language companies use to define workers doesn't necessarily correlate to what role that worker is actually in.

For purposes of understanding rights, TVC workers may or may not have the same protections as their full-time counterparts. If there is ambiguity about whether or not someone is an independent contractor or whether joint-employer rules apply, it is important to double check with a lawyer before including or excluding someone who may or may not be a potential union member.

Protected concerted activities

The final piece of the puzzle in understanding what rights the NLRA grants is understanding what actions the NLRA actually protects. The NLRA protects what it calls "protected concerted activities." We'll discuss this concept by breaking it into two sections – collective action and collective bargaining, though both fall under the umbrella of protected concerted activities.

---

7. https://caselaw.findlaw.com/us-9th-circuit/1297250.html

Collective Bargaining

While the traditional understanding of "collective bargaining" con-jures up images of unions and representatives, the NLRA definition of collective bargaining is actually much broader. The NLRA defines "labor organization" as:

The term "labor organization" means any organization of any kind, or any agency or employee representation committee or plan, in which employees participate and which exists for the purpose, in whole or in part, of dealing with employers concerning grievances, labor disputes, wages, rates of pay, hours of employment, or conditions of work.

In short, a labor organization does not necessarily have to be a formal union. A group in which employees participate and discuss wages, working conditions, and similar topics is a labor organization, and therefore protected under the NLRA. This may seem deceptively broad, but it is not. The NLRA is broad in its protections to give as much power to workers as possible.

Collective Action

From another section of the NLRA:

Employees shall have the right to self-organization, to form, join, or assist labor organizations, to bargain collectively through representatives of their own choosing, and to engage in other concerted activities for the purpose of collective bargaining or other mutual aid or protection, and shall also have the right to refrain from any or all of such activities except to the extent that such right may be affected by an agreement requiring membership in a labor organization as a condition of employment

"Concerted activities" here means exactly what it sounds like. Workers have every right to discuss together their working conditions and wages, and work together to resolve them in a way that benefits them as a collective group. Employers who take steps to forbid this are breaking the law.

To take an earlier example, Shannon Wait discussing wages and working conditions with her fellow workers was protected activity, and her employer could not legally ask her to not discuss bonuses. However, Wait was ultimately suspended for allegedly breaching her non-disclosure agreement (Interview with Shannon Wait, 8 December 2022). Breaching an NDA is not a protected activity, and so they believed they were acting within the law.

However, as Wait's case shows, following the letter of the law does not always mean an employer is acting within the spirit of the law. In her case, her suspension was ultimately overturned when the NLRB found that the NDA reasoning was not the true reason for her suspension. Rather, she was suspended because she had been engaging in protected concerted activity by working with her co-workers to discuss wages and working conditions.

Actions that workers take to protect each other and to stand together are collective actions. They are protected by law. If an employer chooses to break the law by trying to retaliate against or suppress organizers, they are breaking that law, and there are consequences.

When rights are violated – NLRB charges

The decision of what is and is not a violation of a worker's rights to engage in protected concerted activity is up to the National Labor Relations Board (NLRB). In any case where a worker feels their rights have been violated, they are welcome to file a complaint for investigation with the NLRB.

As an example of this process, we can look at my own experience as an organizer in the tech industry. In summer of 2021, I became one of the leaders of #AppleToo, a burgeoning labor movement at Apple. My work with #AppleToo centered around working conditions and understanding the common situations Apple workers had experienced. Working with Cher Scarlett, I worked to collect stories from Apple workers of their experiences with discrimination, harassment, and abuse. The stories included worker after worker who had approached human resources, only to be brushed off, ignored, or retaliated against. I collected hundreds of stories from workers around the company, expressing a wide range of circumstances, but always with the same undertone—the company they believed they worked for and the promises it made of equity and respect was not the company they ultimately experienced.

For some workers, it was enough to share the story and know they were finally being heard and believed. For others, they wanted to take further action and ensure that telling the story would not be the end of the line. I collected legal resources and trusted press contacts, and put those sharing their stories in contact with those who could investigate and share their stories to a broader audience. Others chose to join a new Discord server, one dedicated to gathering Apple workers for collective action. On this server, we planned actions, wrote letters, and decided how we wanted #AppleToo to evolve into a true union. It was in this Discord server, with workers from around the world who had entrusted myself and Scarlett with their stories, that AppleTogether was born.

I was far from the only organizer involved with #AppleToo, and later, AppleTogether. However, most organizers chose to stay anonymous and out of the public eye, making their affiliation with #AppleToo more subtle in internal spaces. I did the opposite. Instead of being anonymous and subtle, I chose to go public with my own experiences at Apple, and become one of the faces of the movement, meeting with the press and managing #AppleToo's media and social media presence. My voice, though not the only voice of the movement, became an easy one to spot and to associate with what was happening with workers at Apple.

Together with my fellow organizers, we drafted an open letter to Apple leadership, asking for improved privacy protections, equitable pay, protection for contract workers and those working throughout the Apple supply chain, and increased accountability from leadership. We gathered hundreds of signatures of support, not only from within Apple, but from across the tech industry in a wave of solidarity.

In September 2021, I sent our open letter to Apple's CEO, Tim Cook, attaching my name and making a very clear statement to Apple leadership that I was working on organizing my fellow workers. Later that day, I was investigated by Apple security, initially having my devices confiscated, then being suspended, and ultimately fired.

Apple's justification for firing me was that I had not co-operated with the investigation, but the timing and context of the investigation gave me reason to believe there was more at play than their stated reasons. With help from an attorney, I filed a charge with the NLRB, alleging that Apple had fired me for engaging in protected concerted action, thus violating the workers' rights outlined in the NLRA.

The process of filing an unfair labor practice charge (ULP) with the NLRB is straightforward, and the NLRB provides excellent guidance for those who choose to file a charge. If you are choosing to file an NLRB charge when you believe your employer has violated the NLRA, I highly recommend speaking to your regional NLRB office. A list of their regional offices is included in the Resources section of this book.

If the NLRB finds in favor of the applicant, it can't issue punitive damages. Rather, it can issue injunctions to prevent employers from taking certain actions, or it can order that a worker be reinstated and backpay provided. It may also require an employer to post public notices about its decisions, or reminders of workers' rights. Its goal is to ensure workers' rights to take concerted actions are protected, and to provide a legal opinion on whether or not that has been done.

It is every organizer's hope that they will not need to file an NLRB complaint. Ideally, everyone's rights would be respected by their employer as they organize their workplace. However, as the thousands of complaints received by the NLRB each year demonstrate, wanting an employer to respect the process doesn't mean an employer will respect the process.

Some of the most common ways employers break the law are:

- Telling workers they are not allowed to discuss their pay or benefits

- Threatening workers for organizing

- Interrogating or investigating organizers

- Promising benefits if workers do not unionize[8]

This is not an exhaustive list. If you believe you have faced unfair labor practices, it is helpful to contact the NLRB for guidance.

Above all else, it's important to remember that the law protects many of the most fundamental elements of worker organizing.

---

8. https://www.nlrb.gov/about-nlrb/what-we-do/investigate-ch arges

Workers have every right to discuss their pay and working conditions with each other, to advocate for one another and stand as one, and to share their thoughts about where they work with the public. When these rights are violated, there is recourse, and that recourse is accessible to anyone, with or without outside legal support. Employers have limits to their power, but it is on the worker and the agencies that support them, to ensure that these limits are respected.

Whether you are an engineer or a call center worker, a founder or a TVC, you have rights. By exercising those rights, you can change your workplace for the better.

State-level Laws

As important as it is to understand the National Labor Relations Act and the role federal legislation plays in the United States, it is also important to keep in mind that the United States' labor laws are a patchwork of state and even local laws that are overseen by a federal system. These state laws cannot violate national law, but that doesn't mean workers in Alabama have the same legal protections as those in California. Knowing the local and state laws that are relevant is critical to understanding what protections organizers have, and what agencies are available to ensure employers follow the law.

There is no clear way to find these laws. While most states record their laws in a legal code, navigating this code can be tedious or difficult. Using third party resources, such as existing unions' guides to state laws, or reaching out to an attorney provides the best summary of local laws.

State and local laws cannot supersede federal law. If an action is protected under the NLRA, it will be protected at a state level. It is in further nuances – such as what role unions play in a workplace, how employers communicate with workers, or what an NDA or employment contract can look like – that the differences start to appear.

Common state laws

Because United States labor law is a patchwork of federal and state laws, it's important to also understand the state-level laws that impact labor organizing. These laws are also frequently changing. It's helpful to keep in mind that each state maintains a legal code that contains all the laws within the state. These are generally helpfully organized into topics, including labor laws. National and state level unions will also generally publish information about changes to state level laws that impact their particular areas, or maintain databases of where these laws can be found. These resources—in combination with local legal advice—can provide a good overview of what laws may or may not apply to you and your situation specifically.

At-will Employment

The first state law to discuss is at-will employment. As of this writing, forty-eight of the fifty states have adopted some version of at-will employment, with Montana and Michigan being the exceptions (Puerto Rico being the other exception, but it, as of this writing, is not a state).[9] At-will employment laws allow employers to fire workers for any reason or no reason at all, unless they are specifically violating a law in firing that worker. This means that employers are within their

---

9. https://sandulligrace.com/the-at-will-employment-rule-is-the
-disease-and-unions-are-the-cure/

rights to, say, fire someone because their favorite color is blue, but not allowed to fire someone because the sacred color of their faith is blue. The latter is illegal discrimination on the basis of religion; the former is not.

The implication of at-will employment is that, for those living in at-will employment states, organizers run the risk of being fired for a "legal" reason as a mask for illegal retaliation. Even if it seems to be clear that the real reason for the firing is because of organizing, at-will employment laws mean it can be difficult to prove, as a true cause doesn't need to be provided.

Public Policy Exemption

There are exceptions to at-will employment laws, though these, again, vary from state to state. All but eight states, for example, have a public policy exemption (see fig. 3.1). In these states, a worker cannot be fired for refusing to do an action that would be against the public's best interests, such as breaking the law or not reporting a safety issue. A worker also cannot be fired for an action that is for the greater good, such as jury duty. An important caveat is that worker organizing, though a societal good, does not fall under a public policy exemption.

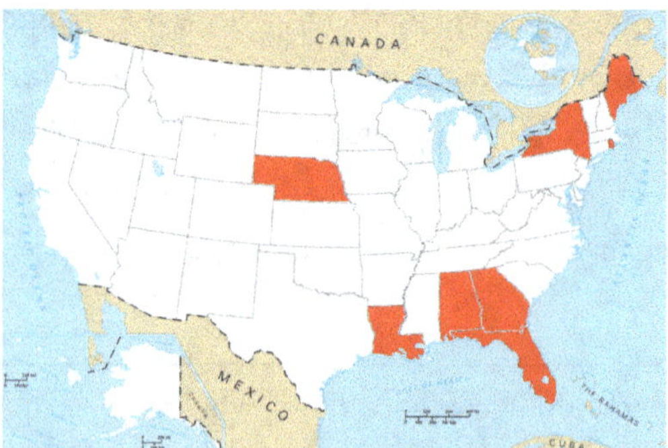

Fig. 3.1: States with a public policy exemption

Good Faith Exemption

Ten states also have a good faith exemption which obligates employers to act in good faith (see fig. 3.2). These laws require employers to provide a truthful reason for why they are firing a worker, and to generally be honest throughout their dealings with the worker. An employer can't provide a series of positive performance review or consistently positive feedback, then fire the worker for poor performance. For them to do so would not be acting in good faith.

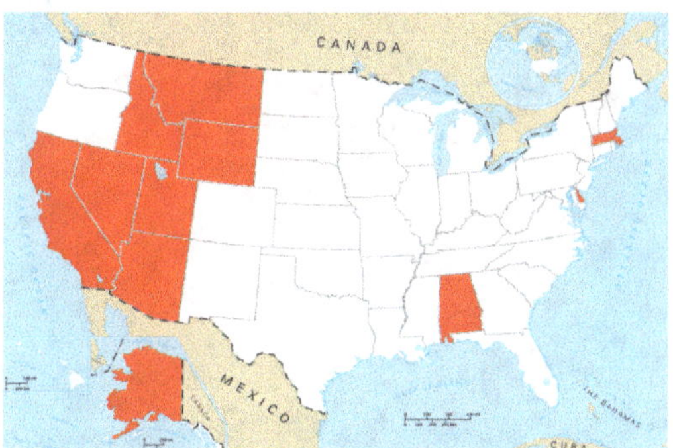

Fig. 3.2: States with a "good faith" exemption

Implied Contract Exemption

Finally, thirty-seven states have an implied contract exemption (see fig. 3.3). Within these states, if an employee handbook or similar document establishes that a worker can only be fired for just cause, or lays out a process by which just cause is established, companies must follow that process.

An example of this might be personal performance plans, common performance pathways which some companies use for workers who are struggling with the expectations of their role. These generally lay out specific goals the worker must meet, as well as specific consequences if the worker does not meet these goals. While these are traditionally used with struggling workers, some companies have also used them to constructively fire workers, either to disguise layoffs, or to manage out workers they would rather not have in their employ. While this exemption looks on the surface like it helps protect workers, in actuality, it provides another vehicle for employers to remove workers under the guise of legal action.[10]

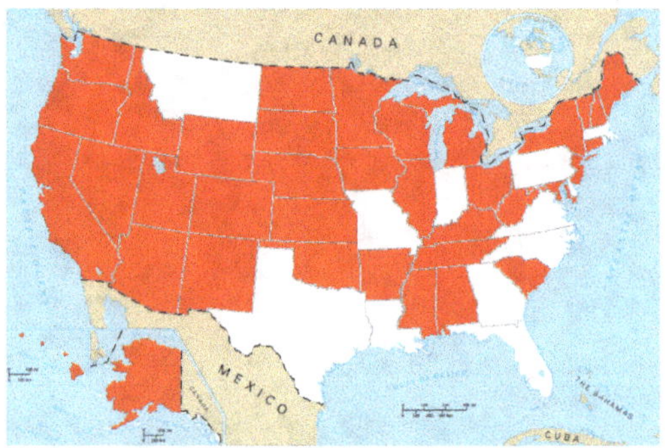

Fig. 3.3: States with an implied contract exemption

How unions help

For workers in at-will states, the primary protection is through unionization. One of the key elements of many, if not most, union contracts

---

10. https://www.paycor.com/resource-center/articles/employment-at-will-laws-by-state/

is to do away with at-will employment, and instead require not only that an employer have just cause, but that a third-party arbiter evaluates the cause to determine if it is indeed valid. Unions not only allow for negotiation of benefits—they can provide a way to ensure that workers keep their jobs and provide a check on employers' power.[11] Unions also provide the resources that, if an employer still decides to fire a worker for what may not be a valid reason, the worker has a legal recourse.[12]

Silenced No More and limitations on NDAs

While laws surrounding at-will employment restrict the power of unions, many states have also begun the process of empowering workers through legislation focusing on NDAs. Numerous states have begun to pass laws banning the use of certain types of restrictive NDAs. In 2018, California passed the Stand Together Against Non-Disclosures (STAND) Act, banning NDAs that forbade workers from discussing settlement agreements involving sexual harassment, assault, or other forms of gender-based discrimination.[13] This law, inspired by the #Metoo movement, prevented workers from being silenced about gender-related discrimination they had faced in the workplace.

---

11. https://sandulligrace.com/the-at-will-employment-rule-is-the-disease-and-unions-are-the-cure/

12. https://work.chron.com/can-labor-unions-employment-coexist-11728.html

13. https://leginfo.legislature.ca.gov/faces/billNavClient.xhtml?bill_id=201720180SB820

Though it was not retroactive, there was a clear recognition about the power NDAs held to silence the truth, and how much of an impact that silence could have.

In 2021, through the work of activists such as Ifeoma Ozoma and Aerica Shimizu Banks, California expanded the protections of the STAND Act in a new act, known as the Silenced No More Act. Rather than being limited to gender-based discrimination, the Silenced No More Act expanded protections to discrimination based on all elements in the California Fair Employment and Housing Act.[14] Under the Silenced No More Act, workers who faced discrimination based on age, pregnancy, race, or any number of protected classes could no longer be forced to sign restrictive NDAs to receive a settlement. Instead, they could tell their stories and discuss their experiences with their colleagues.[15] Their voices were restored, and in doing so, they could begin to hold companies to account.

In 2022, through the work of Cher Scarlett and Chelsey Glasson, Washington passed its own version of the Silenced No More Act, extending the same protections California offered to workers in Washington.[16] Workers in these states could now speak with the confidence that they would not face the financial and emotional cost of lawsuits after telling their stories. Oregon's Workplace Fairness Act went further in making it illegal for an NDA to ban discussion of the

---

14. https://leginfo.legislature.ca.gov/faces/billNavClient.xhtml?bill_id=201720180SB820

15. Interview with Aerica Shimizu Banks, 18 October 2022

16. https://www.protocol.com/bulletins/washington-silenced-no-more

amount of a settlement, in addition to forbidding discussion of discr
imination.[17] As of this writing, similar legislation is being considered
throughout the United States, including in Maine, Vermont, New
York, New Jersey, Maryland, Virginia, Tennessee, Illinois, Louisiana,
and Hawaii.[18]

In 2023, the NLRB further limited the power of NDAs in severance agreements by issuing a memo that severance packages could
not contain blanket non-disparagement agreements or demand that
workers keep the terms of those agreements secret.[19]

Arbitration Agreements

In the slew of documents and forms new employees fill out when
starting a new job, there is usually a document that slips in under the
radar, looking benign for what it is. Most of us have, at some point,
signed an arbitration agreement as part of starting a job. These, too,
are regulated by a patchwork of state laws, though increasingly, also
by federal law.

Arbitration agreements are documents that require workers to resolve their disputes through arbitration rather than through courts.
This system of arbitration generally favors employers, and keeps potentially illegal activities on the part of the employer from ever making

---

17. https://olis.oregonlegislature.gov/liz/2022R1/Downloads/Mea
sureDocument/SB1586/Enrolled

18. https://silencednomore.org/legislation

19. https://www.nlrb.gov/news-outreach/news-story/nlrb-genera
l-counsel-issues mcmo-with-guidance-to-regions-on-severance

it to the public eye.[20] These agreements, by design, suppress workers' voices and disempower workers from seeking justice.

Arbitration agreements, however, do not prevent workers from filing charges with the NLRB, EEOC, or any other regulatory body. That right is always protected, regardless of state law or any arbitration agreement.

State Laws

In light of the power that arbitration agreements have to silence workers' voices, multiple states have passed laws making arbitration agreements null and void in the case of claims around sexual harassment and assault. In New York, Illinois, Washington, and California, arbitration acts no longer prevent people from pursuing legal remedies for sexual assault and harassment in the workplace.[21] Though this is currently limited, much like with the STAND Act being expanded into Silenced No More, it is not unlikely that this legislation will be passed in other states, and expanded to include more forms of workplace issues.

20.

https://www.reuters.com/legal/legalindustry/workplace-arbitra tion-agreements-where-we-are-where-were-going-2022-08-15/

21.

https://www.reuters.com/legal/legalindustry/workplace-arbitra tion-agreements-where-we-are-where-were-going-2022-08-15/

FAIR Act

While no federal legislation currently exists, the Forced Arbitration Injustice Repeal Act (FAIR) would render all arbitration agreements illegal. This would have huge implications for workers' voices and the right to pursue legal remedies in case of illegal employer actions. However, as of this writing, the FAIR Act has not passed the Senate.

Which state's laws apply?

In addition to the complexities of each individual state's labor laws, many workers may be in a situation where multiple states' laws might apply. If a company is headquartered in one state, but the worker works and lives in another, the laws of either state might apply.[22] To go back to my example NLRB charge, though I lived in Texas, Apple is headquartered in California, so my charge was filed in California. I also had the option to file in Texas. However, as California has stronger worker protection laws, I chose to file there instead.

Understanding how different states' laws interact in a particular employment situation gets very complex very quickly. If there is any question about which state's laws you should follow or apply, check with an attorney first. However, even if you live in a state with weak worker protection laws, if your company or boss is somewhere with stronger laws, you may still be protected by those laws.

---

22. https://www.businessmanagementdaily.com/68241/which-state-laws-apply-to-remote-employees/

I have rights!

Though it may not always feel that way, you as a worker have a whole host of rights guaranteed to you by the federal government. You always have the right to:

- Discuss your compensation with your coworkers

- Discuss your working conditions publicly

- Organize and show worker solidarity through buttons, hats, and other actions

- Speak with government agencies, lawyers, or law enforcement

- Organize a union without interference from the employer

In addition, depending on what state you live in, you may also have the right to:

- Receive honesty and truthfulness from your employer

- Not be fired for doing a public good

- Only be fired for cause

- Not be bound by an NDA from discussing your workplace experiences

These rights are constantly growing. As more and more states pass legislation that protects workers' rights to speak and organize, your rights will continue to expand. In the meantime, the NLRB always provides an avenue to speak when your rights have been violated. The law is your ally. Never be afraid to use it.

4. Union busting

As long as workers have been organizing, companies have been working to stop them. The tech industry is no different, with companies following decades-old playbooks and tactics. Even as worker organizing evolves, the use of these strategies is a testament to how effective union busting can be and how effective these tactics can be at dissuading workers from unionizing.

This chapter, like the one before it, will not be a comprehensive list of union busting tactics a company might take. Rather, we'll go through some of the most common approaches and, more importantly, how to respond, both proactively and reactively, to union busting. The best defense for a union against union busting is to know it's coming and inoculate members against it.

A final note before we dive in is that it's important to remember how ubiquitous union busting is. In conducting interviews for this book, not a single organizer didn't experience some form of anti-organizing or union busting behavior. Though companies may differ in their size, structure, mission, or composition, they follow the common theme—unions are not in their best interest and must be stopped. The company you work for is no different. Be prepared, and ensure your fellow workers are prepared as well.

In an ideal world, companies would follow the law and not take action to prevent workers from unionizing. This doesn't preclude management from doing internal audits to understand why a union drive happened, but would allow workers to make up their own minds about unionizing without interference from the company. This rarely happens in practice. Even in cases where a company voluntarily recognizes a union, there are still attempts at union busting before the union reaches out to the NLRB.

Overt Union busting

Overt union busting is fairly common in the tech industry. This manifests through activities like captive audience meetings, firing or disciplining organizers, and rearranging bargaining units so they can no longer organize. Each of these has its own response, and some are illegal under the NLRA. However, as we've seen previously, an act being illegal doesn't necessarily stop a company from trying it, especially when they believe a union is about to successfully form. Penalties under the NRLA are miniscule, whereas unions have the potential to cause issues for companies that treat their workers unfairly. Many companies will take their chances with the NLRB rather than letting a union in.

Captive audience meetings

Captive audience meetings are overwhelmingly common in union campaigns, being held by companies in 89% of union campaigns between 1999 and 2003. They are also incredibly effective at tamping down support for unions, with win rates between campaigns that didn't have captive audience meetings and those that did varying between 73% and 47%.[1] Knowing how to respond to a captive audience meeting can mean the difference between a successful union campaign and an unsuccessful one.

What is it?

A captive audience meeting is a meeting in which leadership presents anti-union talking points to workers. These meetings may be mandatory, and workers may not be able to leave them. They can be held as often as a company wants them to be held, except for 24 hours before an election. As of this writing, mandatory captive audience meetings are considered illegal under the NLRB;[2] however, this ruling has changed, and may change in the future as well. Mandatory captive audience meetings being illegal does not preclude companies from holding voluntary meetings.

These meetings are dangerous specifically because they don't always present the opportunity to have a dialogue. Rather, it becomes a forum for leadership to spread misinformation about unions and what could change in a company with a union. Common phrases include fears that a "third party" will make the business culture different, that there is no guarantee workers will have the same pay or benefits,

---

1. https://onlabor.org/captive-audience-meetings-a-background
   er/

2.
   https://www.nlrb.gov/news-outreach/news-story/nlrb-general-c
   ounsel-jennifer-abruzzo-issues-memo-on-captive-audience-and

or that dues might be inordinately expensive.[3] Leadership may also apologize and offer to do better, or in some similar way use emotion to try to turn the conversation from a discussion of facts to an surge of emotion.[4]

How should I respond?

The best way to counter a captive audience meeting is with facts, both proactively and reactively. Providing union members with information about unions, and addressing the issues that are likely to be brought up during a captive audience meeting beforehand helps inoculate against the misinformation that will be shared during a captive audience meeting.

During some meetings, it may be possible to ask questions. Using the time for questions provides a way to offset the misinformation within the forum in which it was just shared. This also provides an immediate response and shows that organizers have the tools and knowledge to counteract management's position. Responding during a captive audience meeting provides a reactive opportunity to counteract misinformation.

---

3. https://unionbustingplaybook.com/

4. https://www.jwj.org/wp-content/uploads/2014/03/Logan-Consultants.pdf

Retaliation

What is it?

Management may fire or suspend organizers under flimsy justifications. This might manifest as performance concerns, conduct concerns, or any number of reasons, but is ultimately illegal. However, just because this is illegal doesn't mean companies will shy away from it. It can take years for a case to be heard, and even if the company is found guilty of violating the NLRA, the penalties are minimal.

How should I respond?

Ensuring support is in place for any fired workers provides reassurance to other members of the union that, should the worst happen and they lose their job, they will not be without support. Ensure that the work of organizing is distributed rather than being reliant on any one organizer. Even if a key organizer is fired, the work of organizing can still continue.

Filing a charge with the NLRB can also be an effective method to counter-act this type of union busting. Even though this response is reactive rather than proactive for any one organizer, showing the company that you understand your legal rights and recourse can discourage the company from further retaliation.

Reorganizing

What is it?

Companies may also try to rearrange a bargaining unit or argue that members of it are not eligible to vote in a union election. While this strategy is less common in the tech industry, Activision Blizzard attempted to transfer Raven QA organizers out of their bargaining unit to dilute their votes and negate their ability to form a union.[5]

How should I respond?

The decision of who is eligible to vote in a union election is ultimately up to the NLRB. Reclassifying workers as supervisors or rendering them ineligible to vote may also be a violation of the NLRA, as it was in the case of the Raven QA workers.[6] In these sorts of cases, the best course of action is to file an unfair labor practice grievance to the NLRB. While resolving termination cases can take months or years, the NLRB generally acts more quickly with active union elections and can potentially issue a quick ruling on whether or not a company's reclassifications constitute an unfair labor practice.

Ultimately, however, the responsibility for recognizing and responding to companies' attempts to union bust lie not with the NLRB, but with organizers within the union. Without their work,

---

5. Interview with Jessica Gonzalez, 14 October 2022

6. https://www.jwj.org/wp-content/uploads/2014/03/Logan-C onsultants.pdf

misinformation would go unaddressed, or the NLRB would not be aware of practices happening within the company.

Subtle Union busting

It is, understandably, not always in a company's best interests to be overt with union busting. Despite low union membership, a majority of Americans support unions, and see them as doing a public good for workers.[7] A company blatantly and obvious oppressing its workers' rights can receive negative publicity or have their reputation damaged.

However, companies also generally don't want a union within the company. Rather than risk the backlash of an overt anti-union campaign, some companies may try a more subtle approach, sowing division or mistrust and driving the union to tear itself apart.

Instilling a Lack of Trust

What is it?

Companies will often make the argument that a union cannot truly represent workers, or that it only serves to be harmful to the company. One example of this comes from Code for America. When its union efforts became public, management responded through a subtle union

---

7.

https://www.pewresearch.org/fact-tank/2021/09/03/majoritie s-of-americans-say-unions-have-a-positive-effect-on-u-s-and-that -decline-in-union-membership-is-bad/

busting, phrasing their concerns with a union less with the concept of unionizing itself, and more with this particular incarnation of a union. Leadership reminded workers that Code for America relied on donors and grants, and that the presence of a union would potentially impact that funding, and in turn, the public good work they were doing. Having a union would harm not the business itself, but the end users who relied on CfA to create the technology to engage with government services.[8]

One director took an additional step and accused the union of being a "white-led" effort. This element, though on the surface potentially mistakable for an observation and a suggestion to improve organizer diversity, was a form of union busting that relied on the culture of Code for America picking up on the hint and turning away from the union.

However, in this case, the attempt backfired dramatically. Code for America did have people of color as organizers. Rather than the conversation becoming about their absence, the conversation shifted to why people of color felt less comfortable being outspoken about unionizing, and the larger conversation about discrimination in the workplace. This statement rang especially hollow coming from a C-suite dominated by white people. Rather than resonating with socially conscious ideals, workers in Code for America saw leadership trying to use concerns about diversity as a cudgel, and responded with even more support for the union.

---

8. Interview with Ben Calegari, 11 November 2022

How should I respond?

The union responded to these statements by being more introspective and making sure to give people of color as much of a voice as possible, inasmuch as those organizers felt comfortable speaking. Though leadership had, to a certain extent, dug its own grave by attempting to weaponize conversations about social and racial justice, the union organizers did not dismiss these arguments entirely. Instead, they used it as an opportunity to be more representative and inclusive of as wide a group as possible.[9]

For those who are on the fence about unionizing, these questions may seem like good faith efforts to understand. For organizers, however, questions and disingenuous statements provide potentially fertile ground to correct misinformation and provide solid facts about unions and what they accomplish.

"Just Asking Questions"

Companies may also ask disingenuous questions in public spaces, using a lack of knowledge about unions to instill doubt in whether or not a union is a good choice for workers.

What is it?

As one example, consider this post made in an Apple organizer Discord server in response to a worker asking for support in unionizing: *"You should also set up time to speak with your managers...Store leaders are sharing both sides of those learns pretty transparently with team*

---

9. Interview with Ben Calegari, 11 November 2022

member that ask. To be clear, not trying to change your mind via discord, but I do believe you deserve to have all of the information before you and your team dive into this venture. Once your in, it's really hard to get back out."

On the surface, this post can seem like a good faith attempt by one worker to ensure that another worker does their due diligence before starting the unionizing process. However, looking into it more deeply, it becomes clearer that this is an attempt to subtly union bust under the guise of "just asking questions." Going to management to better understand whether or not to unionize is ill-advised. Management's responsibility is to prevent a union, and approaching them provides them with the perfect opportunity to do so.

Leaving a post like this unaddressed, though, still leaves misinformation out there. The best reaction to this sort of misinformation is correct information. A reply to that post provides the perfect counter to that misinformation:

"...Apple is under no obligation to tell the truth, at all....For example, managers can 'predict' that a store will close because of extra costs a union brings. Every conversation we had...was entirely coercive by n ature....Nothing about what management is being instructed to do is factual or unbiased. Nothing during the campaign was truly unbiased and everything since then has been largely retaliatory."

By providing real examples from the unionizing experience, this response demonstrates what management's actual response to unionizing is, and provides a strong disincentive to talking to leadership about unionizing. It also gives future organizers examples of what they'll face when they unionize—that not only is leadership not on their side, but it will actively oppose them, even past the point of legality.

In addition to providing a lived experience from their own union-ization drive, this organizer also provided facts about the good unions can do for workers and workplaces to further solidify why unions matter:

"Union members make, on average, about 11-15% more than non union counterparts. This is higher in some areas.

Integral Healthcare won a pay raise and quarterly meetings with the executive board through bargaining recently.

The issue with what management tells people is that it's a bunch of hypothetical worst case scenarios."

In this response, the organizer not only shows the benefits unions can and have brought, but also what tactics management uses to mask those benefits. These posts are a fantastic counter to the original post suggesting a potential organizer should talk to their manager before organizing. Rather than leaving that point unaddressed, this organizer uses their own experiences to make a response real.

How should I respond?

An easy way to tell if something might be subtle union busting is to consider the source of information. As with all misinformation, if the source of the information has a vested interest in not telling the whole story or presenting a particular image, it may not be the most reliable or unbiased source. If leadership is presenting itself as a source of information about unions or particular organizers, the information they're presenting is likely not the most reliable. Instead, it's helpful to research concerns independently, or to ask questions directly to union organizers. Asking tough and pointed questions is important for making sure the union being built is one that accurately captures everyone's needs. Responding with facts and truth and not letting anti-union messaging occupy the space is the best way to respond to union busting.

Counter-organizing

One of the more insidious forms of union busting, counter-organizing is dangerous specifically because it takes the tactics of organizing and uses them against organizers.

What is it?

Counter-organizing is a form of union busting where a company will spur other workers into taking action against the union organizing, generally by creating division within the company, or leveraging management to organize anti-union committees on management's beha lf.[10]

This particular type of union busting is more insidious because of the emotional toll it can take on organizers and how personal it can get. Organizers have, after all, invested a great deal of effort in ensuring that their campaign is inclusive and captures as many issues as possible, as well as as diverse a body of voices as possible. Getting a strongly negative emotional response to that activism can be incredibly disheartening.

One example of this is from the Oklahoma City Apple Store unionization effort. After an Apple store in Atlanta went public with its unionization drive, organizers in Oklahoma City like Michael

---

10. https://www.jwj.org/wp-content/uploads/2014/03/Logan-C onsultants.pdf

Forsythe began their own drive, centered around pay equity, career development, and safety. The organizers held dozens of conversations with their fellow workers, listening and being empathetic, and following up and standing in solidarity with one another.[11]

As they approached a majority, the Oklahoma City organizers became more aware of Apple's union busting tactics. As they prepared to go public, Michael and his fellow organizers educated each other about captive audience meetings, intimidation, and other tactics. They were aware that they faced an uphill battle, which made it easier to respond to some forms of union busting when they did come up.

However, this sort of inoculation did not make the emotional toll of counter-organizing easier. Once the Oklahoma City organizers went public, multiple of their fellow workers posted on internal social media, lamenting the "divide in the culture." For those who had been on the fence about joining the union, the emotions of these types of posts hit harder, making them worried about the impact the unionization effort was having on their jobs and the community in which those jobs existed.[12]

Michael and his fellow organizers responded by making as many people feel welcome within the union as possible. They highlighted the positive achievements the workers had made, and the commonalities they all held. They responded to the negativity surrounding the unionization effort with positivity and community, reassuring those on the fence that the union would not represent a destruction of their culture, but rather, a new approach that maintained the same social relationships and care workers had for one another. This approach

---

11. Interview with Michael Forsythe, 26 September 2022

12. Interview with Michael Forsythe, 26 September 2022

of being prepared for the counter-organizing and responding with inclusivity was ultimately successful. On 15 October, 2022, workers at the Penn Square Apple Store voted 56—32 to unionize.[13]

How should I respond?

Counter-organizing is successful because it uses the desire to make a difference, and turns that against the organizers. It sows dissent in a union, and feeds on people's inherent desire to be decent to one another.

Being aware of the tactic and inoculating against it is the best way to face a counter-organizing campaign. Putting posts and comments like those in Oklahoma City in context helps make it clear that the emotion expressed, though real, is coming from a union busting space.

Being prepared with facts, and remembering data also helps power through the emotional toll of counter-organizing. Prepare a fact sheet and a common FAQ, but also be aware of high emotions. Don't be afraid to call out union busting for what it is, while still being considerate of workers who do not want a union.

Employee Resource Groups

Though not explicitly a union busting tactic, it's important to understand the role employee resource groups (or ERGs) play in union busting.

---

13. https://www.nytimes.com/2022/10/14/business/economy/apple-store-union-oklahoma-city.html

What is it?

ERGs are groups set-up by the company for traditionally marginalized groups to create a space for members of that group to discuss their shared experiences, share common concerns, and advocate for one another. If this sounds familiar, it's because these are the same sorts of traits you've cultivated in your union. The difference is that a union exists independent of the company, while an ERG exists within and with the permission of the company. It must inherently follow the company's rules, or it will cease to exist.[14]

ERGs provide an opportunity for workers to express their thoughts and frustrations and feel heard. They allow workers to highlight issues and bring them to the company's attention, where the company can then address them. This, in turn, makes workers feel empowered and like they have an impact on the course of their workplace. According to the union busting firm IRI Consultants, making workers feel engaged through these sorts of initiatives is one of the strongest ways a company can "union-proof" their workplace.[15]

Moreover, ERGs can provide an avenue to not only make employees feel heard, but to also suppress organizing before it starts. One example of this comes from Laurence Berland and his involvement with an Alphabet ERG called Gayglers. In 2019, in response to what he saw as insufficient protections from harassment for LGBTQ+ Youtubers, Berland sent an email to the Gaygler ERG, suggesting they organize

---

14. https://www.protocol.com/workplace/employee-resource-gro
    up-weaponization

15. https://blog.unionproof.com/giving-employees-a-voice/

a petition to not march in the upcoming San Francisco Pride parade with the Google contingent. In response, Alphabet made it clear that anyone who protested Alphabet's participation in the parade as part of the ERG would face disciplinary action.[16]

Though the ERG ostensibly existed to benefit workers, it became clear the main beneficiary of the ERG was the company itself. Workers who had previously been interested in organizing and protesting what they say as unequal moderation and protection on Youtube instead became afraid to act.[17] The ERG as a company body had succeeded – worker organizing was suppressed.

How should I respond?

Though ERGs exist to benefit the company, this doesn't mean the people within them aren't necessarily valuable potential members of your union. ERGs succeed because workers believe that speaking within them will lead to action or change, or that their grievances are meaningfully heard. Emphasizing that this isn't the case helps break the spell and make it clear that ERGs serve the company, not the workers.

Providing clear examples of issues that have gone unaddressed by the ERG helps counter the idea that they are pro-worker organizations. Showing how the energy put into ERGs only benefits the company, not workers, can also be an effective way to convince someone to

---

16. Interview with Laurence Berland, 10 October 2022

17. Interview with Laurence Berland, 10 October 2022

channel their energy into an organization that is truly theirs, not the company's.[18]

ERGs are often full of very passionate people wanting to make a difference in their workplace. These are the types of people unions strongly benefit from having in their midst. Showing ERG members how limited the ERG is, and how much more they could accomplish in the context of a union makes the union significantly stronger.

Inoculation, Determination, and some cold, hard facts

Building a union is hard, even without a company's interference. Union busting serves to make it even more difficult. At times, it can be tempting to give up or to believe what the company is telling you. However, with determination, a knowledge of what's coming, and facts about what a union will do for your workplace, it's possible to overcome even the strongest union busting.

Your union will not be the first to face union busting. It will not be the last. In addition to all the steps laid out in this chapter, consider reaching out to another union in a company like yours, or a union you admire and ask them for advice on how they dealt with union busting. Sometimes, just having that solidarity and a little more knowledge can make all the difference.

As you build your union, put together a fact sheet on what unions do so that, when disingenuous questions or captive audience meetings do come up, you have the answers ready to make sure your fellow

---

18. https://theintercept.com/2022/06/07/union-busting-tactics
    -diversity/

workers know the facts. Research union busting tactics ahead of time and educate your members so all of you know how to respond. I've listed the tactics we've discussed below, along with ways to counter them.

- If your company is holding captive audience meetings, respond with facts, probe with questions, and meet with colleagues beforehand to provide information.

- If your company reorganizes, file an unfair labor practice charge with the NLRB.

- If your company retaliates by either firing or suspending organizers, support fired and suspended workers, and file a charge with the NLRB.

- If your company tries to instill a lack of trust, respond with facts and ensure the union is representative, transparent, and democratic.

- If your company engages in disingenuous questioning, respond with facts.

- If your company counter-organizes, inoculate your union members, respond with facts, and be empathetic towards the anti-union workers.

- If your company has employee resource groups (ERGs), emphasize the ERG's lack of power to instill real change.

Above all, though, remember that the company is only fighting for its bottom line. You and your fellow workers are fighting for your whys, those things you hold on to and believe in. What you're fighting for is so much more powerful. Believe in it, each other, and yourself, and you'll make it through.

5. Conversations and how they build unions

The reality of unionizing is that, at its core, it's an activity that requires understanding the why. It requires understanding both what rights you have as well as what obstacles you face. Unionizing is a long series of conversations understanding the whys around you and addressing the concerns about the obstacles in your way. Conversations about rights help move aside the barriers. Conversations about why build solidarity.

This chapter will dive into the specifics of how to have these conversations, who to have them with, and how to do the work of building a union. You will not be alone—there will continue to be examples of other organizers who have done this before, what they learned, and the advice they have to share. Unionizing is the work of building solidarity, and of being empathetic and attentive to those around you. Let this section be the instruction manual of how to finally put those pieces together.

Got your toolkit and a friend handy? Let's build this union together.

Asking Why and Having Conversations

Throughout the book so far, there has been a common theme of voices and the power that a voice holds. Whether it be through speaking up internally, speaking publicly, or any of the other myriad ways one can exercise their ability to speak, your voice is the most powerful tool you have.

In addition, we've also discussed the importance of understanding why. Part of that is recognizing and articulating your own "why," but also, learning, empathizing, and understanding your fellow worker's "why" as well. A huge part of that power comes from the ability to have conversations and build a coalition that raises its voice in unison.

For some, it may seem simple to talk about having a conversation. Conversations, after all, are the bedrock of society. Networking is the foundation on which careers are built, chats the foundation of friendships, talking is what we as humans do. However, organizing conversations are conversations with a specific goal. Before diving in, it's important to understand that goal, and to understand who to talk to and how.

It is also important to emphasize that organizing is not just an action for the gregarious. For introverts, the idea of having a conversation, even with someone you know, can be terrifying or seem impossible. I am an introvert, and one of the hardest parts of being an organizer was working up the courage to talk to someone. While this book can't necessarily provide training on how to make having a conversation easier, it can give a helpful structure for approaching conversations that might make having them a little less intimidating.

The how's of conversation

Before diving into any conversation, it's important to establish who to talk to and where to talk to them. As previously established, discussing a union is legally protected organizing, but it isn't the best idea to have conversations about unionizing openly. Especially in the early phases, it is important to maintain a degree of secrecy around unionizing to get as much work done as possible before the company finds out there is organizing. While we'll discuss more of the specifics of union busting in a later chapter, it's important to keep in mind that companies will take steps to prevent workers from organizing. The more work that's done before the company finds out about the union, the better equipped the burgeoning union will be to handle the company's response.

Because secrecy is important, conversations about unions should not be had on company devices or company property. Company devices and communication spaces—like company Slack channels—are able to be monitored by the company, and so are not secure or secret places to have organizing conversations. Similarly, while breakrooms may seem like good places to have a conversation with a coworker, they are open to everyone, including managers. While it may seem paranoid, being cognizant of the security of a space and who could be listening can give a union valuable time to form.

For workers working in offices, and those who prefer in-person chats, a good way to have conversations safely might be to invite a coworker out to lunch or coffee, or use a shared off-campus activity as an excuse to have a conversation.

For remote workers, or those who prefer remote chats, finding ways to chat without using company resources or space is both more and less difficult. Meeting via Zoom, Google Meets, or any other video conferencing software on a non-company device provides a space to meet that is secure and protected. Setting up a Discord server or private Slack server provides a way to funnel a conversation directly into an organizing instance.

Of course, in addition to the logistics of where and how to have a conversation, a key component of maintaining security is to have a clear idea of who is and is not safe to talk to. As previously discussed, not all workers are covered by the NLRA. Supervisors, managers, and anyone who is in a position where they manage others are not safe to speak to. Similarly, HR, though they may not be in management, are generally not safe to talk to as, once again, their role requires that they protect the company.

A good way to decide who to talk to is through sketching out a conversation map. This exercise helps provide a clear pathway for who to talk to, what paths conversations can take, and how a union can grow from one person to many.

Put simply, a conversation map sets out a series of conversations. To develop one, we organize our work relationships into groups, decide who within those groups to talk to, and set clear and manageable goals for how many conversations to have, and when to have them.

Conversation maps

It seems obvious, but the best people to involve in a unionization campaign are the people who see a union as adding something to the workplace. While you and I know that every workplace benefits from a union, union campaigns flourish more in environments where there is something to rally around. That "why" matters.

Since unionization campaigns work best when people have a reason to unionize, the best people to target for conversations about unionizing are people with a "why." Think about your own workplace. Are there people who are dissatisfied with their working conditions or some aspect of their job? These are people who would likely be more interested in a union.

Similarly, unionization campaigns work better when there are people willing to do the work to make them happen. In your workplace, there are likely leaders who already do the extra work of building the workplace as a social space, or who advocate on behalf of others. There may also be people whom others look up to as examples of what to do. These are also good people to talk to about unionizing.

Let's break down an example workplace to understand who to talk to first and who the best subjects are for conversation. Anita and her team have consistently had bad experiences with pay inequity and a disregard for worker well-being. She believes a union would help alleviate these issues, and is confident many of her colleagues believe the same.

We'll start by breaking Anita's team up into the people who would be best to talk to, those who are less good to talk to, and those Anita should avoid talking to. We'll put each of her coworkers on this chart:

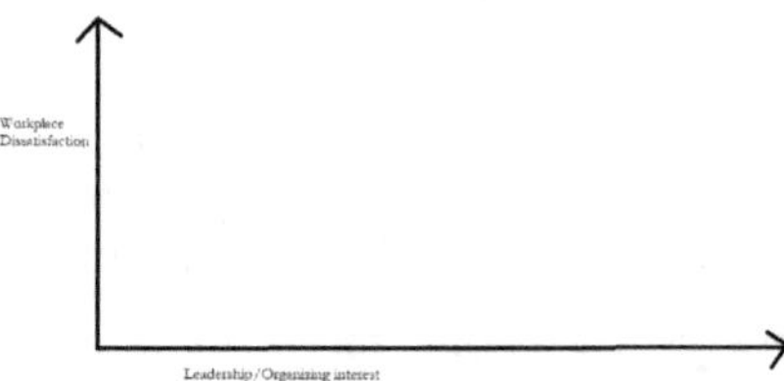

Fig. 5.1: A rough map for how to classify potential fellow organizers

Anita works on a team with three other people—Bartholomew, Cassian, and Daiki—and her manager, Eddie. From her day-to-day interactions with her team, Anita knows that Daiki has been having similar issues with pay equity and discrimination, and has been very willing to talk about his frustrations with their working conditions. They fit here on Anita's chart:

Fig. 5.2: Adding the first potential organizer to the map

Cassian has been frustrated, but tends not to discuss working conditions, preferring instead to focus on her work. She fits here on Anita's chart:

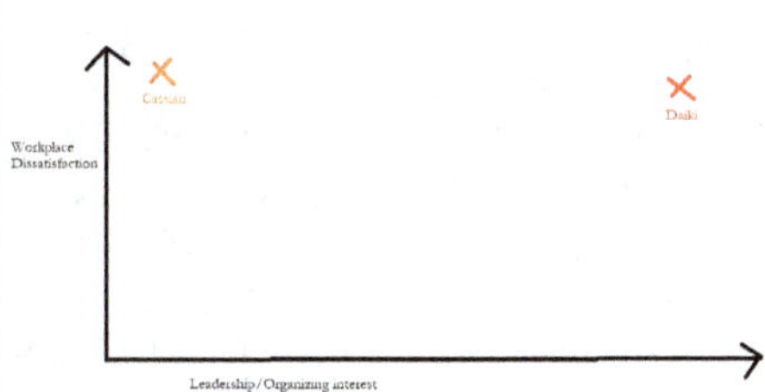

Fig. 5.3: Adding more potential organizers to the map

Bartholomew is very happy with the direction of the team and the company, and thinks Anita is over-reacting to some of management's actions. He fits here:

Fig. 5.4: More conversations lead to more names on the map

Since these are people Anita interacts with every day, Anita's direct coworkers are some of the best starting points for any conversation about unionizing. However, within her team, there are differences in who she should speak to first.

We can already see that, because they are interested in organized and have a strong "why," Daiki is a good person to talk to about unionizing. Cassian, even though she has a strong "why," is not interested in organizing, and so should not be Anita's first conversation. Bartholomew has no "why" and no interest, and so should not be a conversation.

Anita also has a good relationship with her manager, Ed. She knows Ed shares her frustrations and is generally pro-worker. However, because Ed is a manager, he has a legal obligation to tell leadership about any union organizing she is doing. Anita should not speak to Ed about unionizing, and should make every effort to ensure Ed does not know she organizing.

The people on your immediate team are not the only people to talk to about unionizing. You may work in conjunction with other teams, or participate in workplace activities, such as employee resource groups (ERGs), social groups, or even a lunch club. All these spaces where you interact with coworkers are fertile grounds to recruit from. Use this same strategy of mapping out your social spaces to map all the potential conversations in your workplace.

As an example, once Anita maps out all the people she interacts with semi-regularly through ERGs, social clubs, and teams she works with cross-functionally, her chart starts to get crowded with potential conversations:

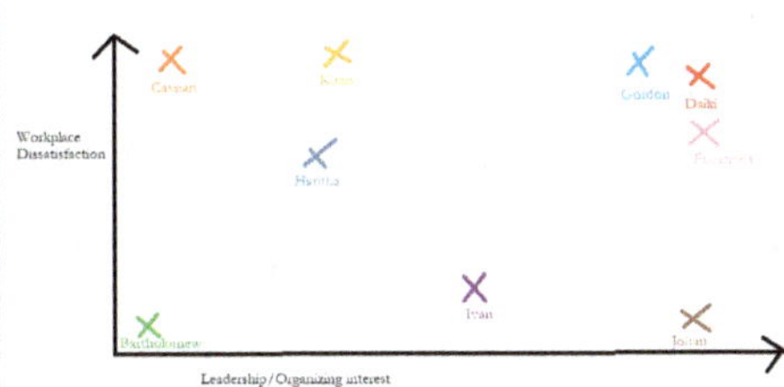

Fig. 5.5: Finishing the initial conversations, the map is full of new potential organizers

The names on the far-right – Gordon, Daiki, Francesca, and Johan – are great people to start with. Gordon, Daiki, and Francesca have strong "whys" and interest in doing something about it. Johan may not have his own "why," but he is motivated to unionize regardless.

From here, the new organizers can make similar charts for themselves. Unions are, after all, a collection of people, and one person cannot do the work alone. By asking others in the group to have conversations as well, the union not only distributes the work of having these conversations, but also creates the likelihood that a person will be spoken to multiple times by different people. Peer pressure and the fear of missing out are powerful forces when organizing. By having multiple people draw a map of their relationships and those they believe they can talk to, a burgeoning union not only gets a strong sense of who should be trusted to join, but ensures they are as excited as possible thanks to the multiple conversations and multiple people they already know to be involved.

What form these conversations take is as diverse as organizers themselves, but there are a few consistent elements that are helpful to keep in mind:

- Secrecy and security are paramount. These conversations should happen off company property and without company equipment. They should also be held with people who are trusted by an organizer. This means that, even if the person is not interested in unionizing, they are unlikely to inform management about any organizing that's going on.

- Start a conversation on something more neutral, like how their week is going, their opinion on a new project or new path the company is taking, or how they feel about their work. Don't be so subtle as to not engage with a meaningful topic, but be sure to pick a topic that can be easily turned to something innocent. Choose what works in the context of your workplace. Think of what, if you were the one being spoken to, might be something you'd like to share with a colleague. For some, that is projects or the company direction, but that isn't always universally true. Choose a conversation starter that offers the flexibility either of turning towards organizing, or turning to a more innocuous discussion about work.

- Be a good listener during these conversations. After asking the opening question, listen carefully to the person's answer. How they phrase their response and what they choose to say speaks volumes to how they feel about their workplace and whether there is anything they'd like to change about it. Not only does this give you an idea of their sentiments, but also whether there is a potential reason for organizing that you and your fellow organizers are not already aware of. Every person's perspective and reasons for organizing are unique, but having a plethora of reasons lays a stronger foundation and some new tendril that future members might be able to latch on to. Listen carefully, and note not only what's said and whether it sounds pro-union, but also for experiences you didn't know your colleagues were having.

- Conversations are the bedrock of your union. Deciding who to talk to and when in the very early stages of unionizing can help determine the course of your union, and if it comes into being at all. Focus on people with strong "whys," and people who are interested. Don't be afraid to reach out to someone new, and to ask questions about people's experiences and motivations. Above all, be empathetic, and remember your why. Each person's experience is unique, and their "why" is as important as yours. Listen, learn, and in doing so, you'll learn to lead.

Using your Why

Another key step is understanding what to say in conversations. Simply going up to someone and asking them if they'd like to form a union is rarely effective. Even saying the word "union" without context can scare people away. Instead, it's important to think about the goal of a conversation. Fundamentally, a union is a long series of answers to the "why" question. Understanding a person's "why" and helping them see how a union would help address it is critical in having effective organizing conversations.

One excellent example of the power of conversations comes from A Better ABK. In July 2021, California sued Activision Blizzard over its workplace culture, and specifically, how that culture discriminated against women and other traditionally marginalized groups.[1] For those working within Activision Blizzard, the issues with the company's culture were already known, but the suit came as a shock nonetheless. Jessica Gonzalez, one organizer within Activision Blizzard, described it as a "mass traumatic event."[2]

In response to the lawsuit, management grew more dismissive of workers' concerns. Rather than addressing the core of the lawsuit, they instead chose to discredit victims and focus on maintaining leadership within the company.[3]

Activision Blizzard, like most tech companies, had a set of ERGs, including a women's ERG. Shortly after the lawsuit by the state of California, Frances Townsend, Activision Blizzard's senior counsel, spoke on behalf of the women's ERG. Her statements did not reflect the beliefs or the experiences of the women in the ERG. Rather, they

---

1. https://www.nytimes.com/2021/07/21/business/activision-blizzard-california-lawsuit.html

2. Interview with Jessica Gonzalez, 14 October 2022

3. Interview with Jessica Gonzalez, 14 October 2022

reflected senior leadership's talking points that discredited victims and the basis of the California lawsuit.

For those within Activision Blizzard, Townsend speaking on behalf of the women's ERG without consulting the members of the ERG was a turning point. There had been attempts to organize before this point; however, they had not been successful. Rather than being supported, organizers worked within a culture that fostered burnout. These previous attempts lost momentum as those spearheading them burned out and left the company.[4]

Townsend's actions changed the conversation. Rather than individuals experiencing mismanagement in isolation, Townsend co-opting the conversation was clear evidence of a culture problem within Activision Blizzard and, more importantly, management's obliviousness to it. There was a clear event that could be used as a rallying cry for change, and a clear outcome that organizers could encourage those around them to achieve.

After Townsend spoke on behalf of the women's ERG, she faced immediate pushback from members of the ERG. Gonzalez and other organizers sent daily e-mails and messages to her, requesting an explanation and some sort of accountability from both her and management as a whole. Their actions culminated in a recorded meeting with over five hundred people.[5]

Initially, the meeting had been intended as a sort of captive audience meeting, where Townsend could explain management's position and stave off the clear worker organizing that was happening within Activision Blizzard. However, it instead became a forum where workers

---

4. Interview with Jessica Gonzalez, 14 October 2022

5. Interview with Jessica Gonzalez, 14 October 2022

could air their grievances to management, knowing they would finally be heard. Person after person shared their story of trauma and their negative experiences at Activision Blizzard. What had been intended as a captive audience meeting instead because a sounding board for trauma.[6]

The power of the moment was not just in finally having a vehicle where management had to listen to its workers for the first time. The power was also in workers finally hearing each other and recognizing that their experiences and their ideas that things could be better were not isolated ones. They could recognize themselves in their colleagues and see themselves in the organizing that was happening around them, and understand the power that such organization wielded over a toxic culture.

Employee organizing at Activision Blizzard only got stronger after the meeting with Townsend. Organizers requested that management share the recording of the meeting, as they believed it provided a powerful example both of what they and their colleagues had been experiencing, and of management's inability to respond in a meaningful way. When management refused to provide the recording, Gonzalez and other organizers held leadership accountable through persistent e-mails and pings, asking for the recording. When it still failed to manifest, they organized a walk-out, sending a clear signal both of how many workers were now part of their movement, and what they were willing and able to do when faced with intransigence and toxicity on the part of management.[7]

---

6. Interview with Jessica Gonzalez, 14 October 2022

7. Interview with Jessica Gonzalez, 14 October 2022

At the heart of their accomplishments, though, lies the power of conversation and of having a central moment that turns a gentle snowfall into an avalanche of worker action. Within Activision Blizzard, organizers' conversations gained power when they could put organizing in the context of a highly unpopular action. Both the lawsuit and Townsend's response to it provided a common ground for organizers and workers, establishing something that created a common rallying cry. Workers who might not ordinarily see themselves within a union could see themselves taking action within a toxic culture. Conversations at Activision Blizzard centered around that, and turned what had been a floundering culture of organizing into a dragon. Voices, workers' voices, became the most powerful thing at Activision Blizzard, and changed not only their company, but the gaming industry as a whole.

While a rallying moment is helpful, it isn't always necessary. Depending on the particular company, there can be different ways to forge a common ground between workers. Code for America is an excellent example of how using an organization's own beliefs and missions can create just as powerful a momentum for unionizing.

Code for America (CfA), unlike other examples we've discussed, is not a for-profit company. It is instead a mission-driven non-profit, focused on making government services as accessible as possible.[8] Its workers tend to be more politically active than in other tech companies, and more cognizant of how systems can exacerbate inequities unless addressed.[9] Workers at CfA also presented an image of being there because of their love for the meaningful work they were doing.

---

8. https://codeforamerica.org/about-us/

9. Interview with Ben Calegari, 11 November 2022

As a non-profit, CfA's compensation was not necessarily as high as other companies, but the knowledge that the work was doing substantive good meant that some workers were content with these lower wages.[10]

CfA did not have a particular inciting event for its unionizing efforts. Rather, after Kickstarter unionized in 2020, workers at Code for America began discussing unionizing less as a way to address a workplace grievance, and more as an exploration of what was possible within a unionized workplace. For Code for America workers especially, the prospect of being more involved in the guiding principles and direction of the company fit their perception of what Code for America strove to be and how it presented itself to the world.

Without an inciting event, the conversations within Code for America instead focused around unionizing as a concept and assessing how people felt about unions within one-on-one conversations. The reasons people were reached out to were as varied as the people themselves. Ben Calegari, one organizer at Code for America, was reached out to because he wore a "ban billionaires" t-shirt in a meeting. Organizers used their knowledge of their workplace and the people within it to make decisions about who was most likely to be interested in unionizing.[11]

Over the course of these conversations, however, organizers found that Code for America was not as equitable as it claimed to be. Higher paid roles were dominated by cis white men, while lower paying roles with harder working conditions were dominated by women and people of color. Though CfA presented itself as valuing equity and

---

10. Interview with Ben Calegari, 11 November 2022

11. Interview with Ben Calegari, 11 November 2022

equitable participation in government services, organizers within CfA found that its pay structure and management culture didn't reflect this. Though they hadn't started with any particular inciting moment, their conversations and listening to each other painted a clearer picture of each individual's "why," and how those individual why's created a larger mosaic. Even if CfA didn't have the same toxic culture of other tech companies, there was still room to make it a more equitable workplace for everyone.[12]

In both cases, organizers used their why to share their experiences with those around them. Their fellow workers, in turn, shared their own experiences, creating a shared narrative. It was this shared narrative, one created with everyone's shared voices, that propelled the movement forward. Voices, speaking their truths, were powerful enough to drive each other, and to drive their employer to change.

This is the power of conversation. Conversation can center both on an inciting moment, or be an exploration of working conditions. Until an organizer actually sits down to have a conversation with a colleague, it's impossible to know what their working life actually looks like. Conversations with a wide variety of people give that clearer picture. They make it possible to understand a workplace from a wide variety of perspectives, and with that, how a union can improve life for everyone.

The Content of Conversations

It's one thing to talk about the power of conversation, but it's important to understand how to have a conversation as well. Effective organizing is based on having effective conversations, and at the core

---

12. Interview with Ben Calegari, 11 November 2022

of those lies understanding whether both parties are interested in a union, and why.

A colleague will rarely answer a question about how work is going with an immediate affirmation that they would like to unionize, though it is helpful if they do. Instead, listen for sentiments about wanting the workplace to change or being discontent with how things are going. If someone is talking about how they believe the workplace is toxic, or if they're frustrated with getting passed over for advancement, bonuses, or pay increases, these are good indications that they would be open to unionizing. Even if the other person isn't being overt, guiding the conversation towards these topics can provide a powerful insight into the person's lived reality.

On the other hand, if the person responds to questions about work and management decisions with strong pro-management sentiments—such as by praising recent decisions or being resistant to the idea that elements of the workplace might need changing—that's a good sign that the particular person should not be made aware of the union. Instead, the conversation should be shifted away from union topics.

Most likely, a conversation will fall somewhere between these two extremes, with the person maybe being reserved about discussing their working conditions in detail, but still sharing some elements that they would like to see changed, or some general sentiments that lean towards organizing. It's in these conversations that listening and guiding the conversation towards unions is most helpful. Even in these conversations, the person will express some reason for why they believe what they do, or what experiences they've had. Listening to these reasons and connecting with your own is critical. In making these connections and forging commonality in the shared experience, it's easier to establish how the union goal you're working towards benefits your co-workers as well. For any movement to be successful, people need to see themselves within it. Showing your fellow worker how a union would help alleviate some of their workplace issues, or bring about the changes they'd like to see will help bring more and more workers on board for the union.

It is also possible to prepare for some of the most frequently asked questions. While each workplace is unique, some fundamental questions will crop up time and time again. Organizers at an Apple store in Florida, upon realizing they were facing similar questions in their conversations, put together a Google doc with those questions and a best answer for them. Not only was this doc shared within their unionization campaign, it was quickly shared with Apple stores globally, creating a powerful shared document with reliable answers to common questions.[13]

Again, every workplace is unique. However, having a common repository can be a good way to provide confidence and knowledge to counter misinformation. Some questions and answers you could include in your repository are:

- Why are you unionizing?

- What is a union?

- Aren't unions just for workers who don't get paid well?

- Why don't we just talk to leadership?

- Can my employer retaliate against me?

- How will dues work?

---

13. Interview with anonymous Apple store worker, 21 November 2022

- Why should I care about a union?

Finally, organizing doesn't solely have to be the realm of extroverts. Through the use of question repositories and the repetition of conversation, through active listening and focusing on someone else's why, the steady stream of conversations becomes a torrent that flows to a sea of change. Though it may seem as though having conversations is solely the realm of those who are already adept at networking, it doesn't have to be. A union is as unique as those building it, and that includes those who aren't traditionally the most active voices in the room

Reviewing your toolkit

Conversations are the backbone of organizing, and unionizing your workplace is no different. When considering starting a union, draw a diagram of your relationships within your workplace, like the ones we've done in the previous pages. List out the people you know, and divide them into likely union organizers, possible union organizers, and definitely not union organizers. Much like with Anita's example, how people are divided can be based on what they do, what they've said, or your experience with them. You know your workplace better than anyone—use your experience within it to decide how best to categorize those you work with most closely.

Having a map or chart gives a clearer sense of what work needs to be done and helps structure organizing. Knowing and thinking critically about who to talk to also provides a series of milestones that ensure there is always the sense that progress is being made. Unions may be made of conversations, but they're fueled by the drive to change things and make forward progress. Having a list of where you're headed next provides tangible steps and the ability to show the progress you're making.

Also take the time to develop your own FAQs for your upcoming conversations. Think about the specifics of your workplace. What are the whys you've encountered so far? How would having a union help them? What fears have people shared about having a union? You can use the information you already know to lay the foundations for all the conversations you're about to have.

Above all, remember that you can do this. A union is all about voices. It is, at its heart, a collection of those voices, speaking in unison. Your first step is just to coax them to utter their first words.

6. Organizing Committees and Union Structures

It's not possible for a single person to organize a union. Instead, the work of unionizing gets divided between members of the burgeoning union. It is in these early moments where the organizing committee and structure of the union begin to take shape.

Bear in mind that the type of company you're in to a certain degree informs what form your union can take. A company with thousands of people won't necessarily be able to have a traditional union, nor will a tiny company benefit from a solidarity union. However, the decision of what kind of union you have ultimately falls to the organizing committee.

In this chapter, we'll discuss not only organizing committees and what they are, but the different forms a union can take and why having a representative, transparent, and democratic organizing committee is so important. Your voice informs the course of your union, but it's the organizing committee that helps transform that voice into a movement.

Organizing Committees

An organizing committee (or OC) is the heart of the organizing effort. Generally comprised of 10-15% of the bargaining unit, it ideally represents a diverse group of the organizing workers, but should at least have a variety of viewpoints within it.

- The organizing committee drives actions forward and makes strategic decisions about what actions to take, where to focus efforts, and who to speak to next.

- If the union is working with any outside national unions or liaising with other unions in solidarity, the organizing committee generally takes the lead in those communications.

- The organizing committee also ensures there is structure in a union. They might allocate work to certain members, decide how work should be distributed, decide whether or not to take an action, or just be available as a first stop for anyone new to the union.

- When the union is meeting as a group, the organizing committee generally leads these meetings and ensures they stay on topic. They are the leaders of the union, and help ensure the collective actions that organizing workers take are effective and coordinated.

- Finally, the organizing committee also keeps track of how the union is doing. They take the lead in deciding when and how to become public with your organizing efforts. In the case of traditional unions, this includes keeping track of how many workers support the union.

This is not to say that the OC are the only members of the union who decide the course of the union. Unions are a democratic organization, and as such, all members should have a say in the course of the union. However, having an OC generally provides more organization and a core that helps keep everyone on track.

Let's look at Anita's case from the previous chapter and how her union is progressing, once she has conversations. Over the course of having conversations, Anita has found that some of her colleagues are interested in forming a union. Those conversations also gave her a greater insight into who to talk to. Her conversations have also successfully yielded others who are now willing to take on some of the work of having conversations. Anita's conversation map is now no longer just the people in Anita's orbit, but is starting to resemble much more of a web (see fig. 6.1).

Fig. 6.1: Anita's proto-OC

Rather than having the OC all come from one team or department, you should have a diverse OC. Part of the purpose of the OC is to facilitate recruitment from a wide variety of teams as effectively as possible. By diversifying the OC, it not only becomes easier to recruit widely, but is more representative of the variety of experiences and issues that each team faces.

For Anita's workplace, she, Daiki, and Kiran quickly identify members from almost every team they work with who they believe would be effective at helping guide the course of the union forward. For example, they think about who tends to take the lead in projects, and who other workers turn to for help. They use their knowledge of their company to identify who would have a strong positive impact and the reputation to push the union forward.

However, they also recognize that unionizing is a lot of work, and they pay attention to who brings energy and ideas to the table. Though others may not have the same workplace clout, these fellow organizers who are excited and passionate about the union are also great candidates for the OC.

After discussing as a group, the new union chooses a diverse combination of people to be the new OC. This OC represents a broad range of leadership styles, opinions, and roles at the company, ensuring as many voices and viewpoints are contributing to the conversation as possible. Their union now looks like figure 6.2.

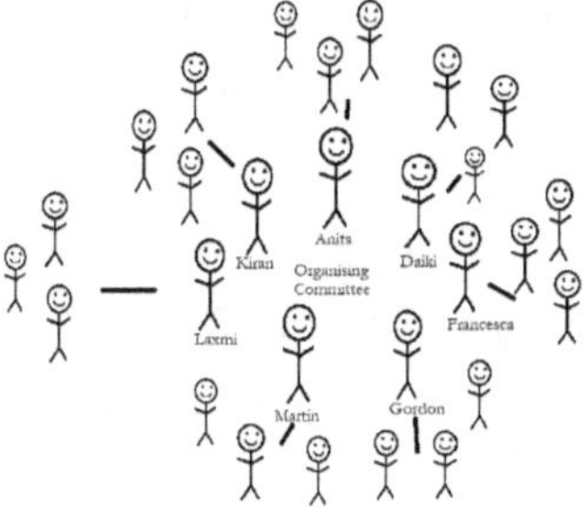

Fig. 6.2: Anita's union with an OC

Each leader brings their followers in and continues to have conversations and drive organizing forward. Recruiting leaders from diverse organizations also shows how the process of unionizing can move much more quickly. It would be incredibly difficult for Anita to have all these conversations on her own. By distributing the work of organizing to a group, the process of reaching as many workers as possible gets easier.

However, there is a tricky balance between forward progress and security.

The Pace of Organizing

Even at this stage, when a not insignificant portion of the company's workers are now involved in the union, security and secrecy are still of the essence. As a result, organizing can sometimes seem to be a long, slow slog with no forward momentum. How long a particular union takes to organize is a product both of its circumstances, and the cautiousness of its members. It can take over a year for a union to go from those first few conversations to announcing, largely because the danger of a company response demands cautiousness.

One example of this comes from Code for America. Despite being a fairly small company—at the time of interview, its staff was around two hundred people—CfA spent over a year organizing its unionization campaign. While this is not in and of itself an abnormally long timeline, because it organized during the pandemic, its workforce was entirely remote. As Ben Calegari, a member of their OC describes it, the lack of physical presence coupled with the slow forward progress meant there could be a sense of "doldrums of inactivity without the warm fuzzy feelings of solidarity."[1]

CfA's union chose to move slowly. Rather than adding people quickly, the OC would add one to two new members per week. For those within the burgeoning union, this progress sometimes felt painstakingly slow. It also meant that, paradoxically, the union could also be exposed to additional risk as members "lost faith" with the union, or got promoted to management in the time the union was organizing. However, when they finally did announce, management had not known they were organizing. Their care meant that they were able to organize without significant interference. It wasn't until after they went public that they faced union busting.[2]

Striking the balance between action and cautiousness is important. Being too cautious can cause people to lose patience and leave the movement. Being too aggressive exposes the movement to management and potential union busting. This is especially true of remote workplaces, where it can be harder to keep the faith that the union is making forward progress when organizers and other workers can't be seen making that progress. Keeping workers engaged and believing in the union allows for cautiousness without creating undue risk.

How you strike that balance depends on the particular company you are organizing within, and the particular union you are building. Having weekly meetings in a secure space, like a Discord server, with announcements of updates and discussion of potential actions provides a good way to keep members engaged. Assigning tasks and getting check-ins from each other also gives everyone the sense that

---

1. Interview with Ben Calegari, 11 November 2022

2. Interview with Ben Calegari, 11 November 2022

there are tangible actions being taken, and that they can contribute to them. Even something small, like designing buttons or graphics, gives everyone the feeling that a union is more than just their conversations, that it is instead a movement that everyone is contributing to.

Types of Unions

There are huge variations in size of companies in the tech industry. From a start-up of a dozen people to a multi-national giant, the tech industry spans a huge range of groups, sizes, and areas of expertise. Much as with everything else in this book, this diversity of structure means that there is no one-size-fits-all solution for what a union in the tech industry looks like. Instead, this variety means that organizers need to make a decision about what form their union will actually take.

Traditional Unions

The most common image of a union is one created through an election, with a bargaining committee, sitting across from the table with a business' leadership, hammering out a contract and representing workers in their employment issues. This model of union holds a great deal of power, and is the model for two of our example cases—Kickstarter and Code for America—use.

This type of union uses a contract (or collective bargaining agreement) between the labor union and the employer to legally define and protect workers' rights in that company. It is the workers in the union who decide what to prioritize in these contracts, whether it be compensation, job security, or work-life balance. These contracts, though negotiated, hold the employer to standards workers find more fair, and help balance the unequal power between workers and employers.[3]

However, for this type of union to come into being, it must either receive voluntary recognition from its company—as was the case with Code for America—or win a union election—as was the case with Kickstarter. These elections rely on a majority of workers in a particular company or bargaining unit voting in favor of a union. This is much simpler for small companies than with larger ones, and much simpler for companies with workforces generally located in a single area rather than being spread out.

One example of how this process of union elections can work in a larger company comes from Raven Software. Raven Software is a subsidiary of Activision Blizzard, and the primary developer of the Call of Duty series. Its quality assurance team is part of a legion of QA contractors at Activision Blizzard, working on a variety of projects.

In December 2021, Activision laid off at least a dozen QA contractors, after having asked some of them to move to Madison, WI, or promised others pay raises. A few days later, the remaining members of the QA team went on strike, walking out in solidarity with their colleagues who had been laid off.[4] While they were on strike, the workers reached out to Jessica Gonzalez and ABK Workers Alliance for support and guidance on how to form a union.

Gonzalez, as one of the organizers of ABK Workers Alliance, had significant experience and knowledge of how to help the Raven QA workers organize. She organized a GoFundMe to establish a strike

---

3. https://guide.unitworkers.com/whatsinaunioncontract/

4. https://www.ign.com/articles/the-entire-raven-software-qa-unionization-story

fund for the workers, raising over $350.000 to ensure the workers could stay on strike for as long as it took to form a union.[5] The workers connected on Discord, then further connecting with Code-CWA for more formal support in forming a union. They sent a letter to Activision Blizzard with their demands—all members of the Raven QA team, including those that were laid off, must be granted full time positions.[6] When Activision Blizzard responded in January by reiterating what it had already stated about its commitments to the workers, the workers formed the Game Workers Alliance (GWA). Despite union busting from Activision Blizzard, Raven QA and the GWA succeeded in forming a union. In May 2022, Game Workers Alliance won its union vote 19 to 3, becoming the first North American video game union at a AAA company.[7]

Though they were contractors for a larger company, they were recognized as a unit because of their shared employer and shared responsibilities, and were eligible to form a union. Rather than trying to hold an election in the much larger Activision-Blizzard, they instead organized as Raven QA.

Raven QA also demonstrates how TVC workers can organize. Rather than organizing as part of their overarching company, TVC workers have the opportunity to organize as workers of their particular employer. Though this does not preclude them from the risk of union busting by either their direct employer or the overarching company,

---

5. Interview with Jessica Gonzalez, 14 October 2022

6. Interview with Jessica Gonzalez, 14 October 2022

7. https://www.polygon.com/23137782/raven-software-activisi on-blizzard-qa-union-win

this does provide them the opportunity to organize on their own terms and with the protection offered by a contract.

While larger companies can be broken up into smaller units that then petition for recognition on their own—as is the case with the Raven QA workers—this process can be prohibitively tedious, especially once the company realizes this is what workers are doing and cracks down. However, for those in large companies who want the protection a collective bargaining agreement offers, breaking into smaller subsets may provide a pathway to recognition.

For those in smaller companies, the path is much clearer. If a majority of eligible workers in the company vote for a union, there can be a union.

Solidarity Unions

Instead of breaking larger companies up into smaller bargaining units, one alternative union format is the solidarity union. This is the structure used by organizers at Apple and Activision-Blizzard. In this style of union, the union itself has no formal agreement with its company. There is no election, no bargaining committee, and potentially no meetings with the company. The company may not even acknowledge its existence. Instead, a solidarity union derives its power from workers choosing to give it power and work together within it in a series of actions. It is not through any formal agreement that the union and its actions gain power, but rather through workers all agreeing to support one another and take action together, hence the term "solidarity union."

This type of union is especially effective in very large companies, such as FAANG companies, and companies with workforces spread out across huge geographical distances, or with widely disparate work assignments. This type of union also grants better flexibility for workers in what would traditionally be very different bargaining units with different interests to better support one another, through supportive action or through participating in the same actions together. Collective actions and organizers within solidarity unions are still protected by Section 7 of the NLRB, meaning they still hold a great deal of power.

One example of this can be seen with actions taken by AppleTogether. With over 130,000 workers, organizing Apple through a traditional union would be nearly impossible. Instead, AppleTogether forms itself as a solidarity union. Its OC makes decisions about how best to and where to focus on unionizing Apple stores, connecting them with one another as well as with national unions. It uses its platform as a solidarity union within one of the world's largest companies to amplify issues, granting national and sometimes international attention to what might otherwise have never been seen.[8] For organizers like Megan Mohr, this space and flexibility of actions also provided the opportunity to blow the whistle on corporate misbehavior, further spurring the effectiveness and power of AppleTogether and its ability to elicit change within Apple.[9]

However much power it may have, a solidarity union does not have formal power, nor the rights a collective bargaining agreement provides. When organizers are faced with termination by the company, these sorts of unions do not have official power to intervene. Instead, they can choose to take an action in response, but whether that action has an effect is ultimately up to the company. The lack of a contract

8. Interview with Laurel Degutis, 2 October 2022

9. Interview with Megan Mohr, 18 October 2022

gives a solidarity union flexibility in what it chooses to do and the steps it chooses to take, but does not necessarily grant security in the way a traditional union does.

Minority Unions

One other increasingly common option, especially in large companies, is the minority union. This type of union does not represent a majority of workers, nor does it necessarily aspire to. It also is not protected by a collective bargaining agreement, though it does still enjoy many of the rights of a traditional union. It also does not have to limit itself in its membership, being able to accept anyone who chooses to join it, and then extending the union's protection to those members who do join. A minority union accepts dues from its members, and uses these dues to fund its actions and any potential legal fees, much like a traditional union.[10]

This is the structure used by the Alphabet Workers Union. Much like with a solidarity union, this type of union does not have formal power or recognition. However, its inclusivity of membership and access to funds means it does have the power to defend its members, set-up strike funds, and put pressure on the company to change. The lack of a contract also grants flexibility in the actions it can take, but does not provide the same protections as a traditional union. For large companies, a minority union may be a good option to ensure there

---

10.

https://www.gtlaw.com/en/insights/2021/2/published-articles/the-rise-of-minority-unions-social-movements-tech-giants-showing-signs-of-things-to-come is some sort of support for workers interested in a union while also recognizing the unlikelihood of achieving a majority vote. Minority unions are also good options in smaller companies that are unable to build support for a traditional union, but whose yes voters still want some sort of collective protection.

Alternative Forms

One potential compromise between these models might be found in United Tech and Allied Workers (UTAW) at Apple. UTAW at Apple strikes a balance between being a majority union and a solidarity union. Originating in an Apple store in London, UTAW at Apple originally followed a traditional union course of gathering members in preparation for formal recognition. However, rather than viewing management as adversarial, workers in London instead announced their activities early, framing it as an opportunity for collaboration with management. These workers established themselves as mediators in workplace grievances and disciplinary action between workers and the company. They worked as well to establish management as former workers, and draw a clear relationship between current workers and management, creating an atmosphere of camaraderie that mitigated union busting.[11]

However, this style of union, while more powerful than solidarity unions, also has its limitations. It is able to be part of the grievance process because leadership allows it to be, rather than because it has a legal right to be. Its cultivation of a positive environment also means it is more limited in the actions it can take. Taking a hostile action, for example, would disrupt the careful balance it strikes and lead to

---

11. Interview with Edwin, 21 October 2022

union busting or the dissolution of the union. This form of union also becomes vulnerable if leadership is no longer willing to tolerate its existence. After asking for more formal recognition, UTAW at Apple experienced union busting, with workers being banned from discussing unions on company property, holding captive audience meetings, and firing a union organizer.[12]

Other Resources

Being engaged with a larger, national union is also helpful for keeping up morale and maintaining the legitimacy of the union. While not necessary, working with a larger union can also provide support and guidance, and take some of the infrastructural work off the shoulders of organizers so they can instead focus on actions within their workplaces. Organizations like CODE-CWA, AFL-CIO, OPEIU, and UTAW in the United Kingdom have experience working specifically with tech workers. Other organizations, like the Emergency Workers Organizing Committee provide guidance specifically on non-majority unions, which are more prevalent in large tech companies. All of the above organizations also provide extensive training for organizers, giving each organizer the confidence to move forward in a clear and planned way.

Engaging with a larger national union isn't necessary for organizing. It is entirely possible to build a union on your own without this support. However, attending some trainings can be immensely helpful, and doesn't require committing to a particular union, or even committing to the idea of unionizing your workplace.

---

12. Interview with Edwin, 14 February 2023

These larger unions generally do not interfere with your internal union structure, instead providing support and guidance rather than direct instructions of who should be in your OC or what form your union should take. They may have some of their own ideas, but the decision is largely yours as to what form your union takes, even when working with a larger union.

If you do decide to work with a national union, I also highly recommend doing your research on the union and making the best choice for your organization. Not all unions are the same, and while your union will still be your own, understanding what being affiliated with each union might mean for your union is important. Don't be afraid to ask union representatives tough questions, and to say no if they are not a good fit.

What structure is right for me?

Which form of union you choose to pursue is partly informed by the company you are in. Large companies leave few options beyond dividing into smaller units or forming a solidarity or minority union. However, for smaller companies, more options provide more possibilities. Understanding your fellow workers', their amenability to unionizing, and the shape of the company helps determine what type of union you might form. All are valid, even if what they do is different. Ultimately, any body that creates the opportunity for workers to come together and advocate for one another is valid and better than nothing at all. It's up to you and your fellow organizers to decide what shape that ought to take.

Before moving on, take a moment to think again about your why and what you hope to achieve with your union. Are you hoping to change elements of company culture or a company value? If so, a solidarity or minority union might be able to exert that power without the need for a collective bargaining agreement. Do you want to improve your working conditions or compensation? The protections and guarantees of a collective bargaining agreement provide a much stronger foundation. What you're fighting for informs what structure works best for you and your fellow workers.

Think about the size of your company and your coworkers as well. If you work in a large company, or if your fellow workers are not particularly amenable towards unions, a traditional union may not be a feasible option.

Consider your company and your why as you review it. Knowing ahead of time what goals are feasible for your organizing helps you plan the actions that will best reach those goals, and allow you to set reasonable expectations for everyone working together to unionize. Also remember that your ideal structure may not be any of these. It is always possible to take something from each structure to build a union that is uniquely yours. You and your fellow workers are ultimately the arbiters of what shape your union takes.

7. Collective Actions

One of the bedrocks of union organizing is collective action. Collective action makes clear to companies how much power workers have, and what consequences a business can face to productivity or its public image when they choose to exercise that power.

Collective action is the term for any action that workers choose to take in conjunction with each other. This can be anything from a strike or a walkout to filing shareholder proposals or working together to change policy. There is a vast range of actions that can be done in support of a union, with the appropriateness of each solely dependent on the union, its members, and what they choose to do. The type of company you work in also informs the effectiveness of certain actions.

It's also important to consider whether and how to publicize the actions you're taking. The press can be a powerful tool, but also reshape a union in unexpected ways. Be prepared for its impact, and decide from the outset how and whether to engage with media and social media.

Because of this variety, and because there is no set list of actions to take—if any—it's most helpful to provide a few examples of actions and the contexts in which they might be taken. This is not exhaustive, and once again, the appropriateness of actions is entirely contingent on the context in which actions are taking place.

The importance of controlling the narrative

In discussing how to prepare to be an organizer, we've talked about the importance of controlling your personal narrative and ensuring your personal "why" doesn't get distorted. As the union grows, those principles still hold true, albeit on a larger scale. Rather than being about you personally, as you take collective actions, ensure that your union's "why" stays true to what the union believes, rather than what others might ascribe to it.

Before taking any actions, ensure that everyone agrees on what the action is meant to achieve, why you are taking the action, and what talking points you will use throughout. Be prepared for questions and for backlash, but don't take it personally. People will always have questions. Answering them in good faith and with consistent answers shows that you and your union are prepared and firm in what you believe.

Much like with your individual "why," not having a solidly defined and controlled narrative dilutes the power of your message. Before taking any action, agree on the "why" and hold to it.

Types of Actions

Part of what propels a union forward and keeps its members motivated is actions. Actions allow unions to demonstrate to a company their members' commitment to goals, and also allow workers to achieve goals while building their union. Actions provide a way to make a statement and back up convictions with demonstrable proof of workers' resolve.

There are a wide variety of actions available, with each being more or less appropriate depending on your goal, your company, or your union's membership. When choosing an action to take, consider the outcome you want to achieve, what needs to be done to convince someone of your argument, and how many people you believe you can involve. Above all, make sure the decision and strategy for actions is made as a group, and that there is buy-in from as many members as possible. A poorly chosen action can cause divisiveness, and potentially fracture a burgeoning union.

Open Letters

One of the most common actions a union can take is an open letter or a letter to fellow workers discussing why workers are organizing. An open letter is most commonly addressed to company leadership and is inviting signatures, while a letter to coworkers might be more direct, through being either e-mailed to the entire company or posted in a general message board, like a Slack channel.

What are open letters good for?

Letters provide a way to communicate goals and motivations in a clear and public way. They remove ambiguity from what a union is doing and why, and provide a way for fellow workers to better engage with the union. Open letters have the added benefit of generally inviting signatures, which provides a good way to gauge support for the letter's contents.

Open letters may also contain a call to action for company leadership. How leadership responds to an open letter also communicates to workers how leadership might respond to worker requests more generally. Leadership taking action based on an open letter may stymie a union, but does ultimately improve working conditions and demonstrate the power of collective action. Leadership refusing to address the letter may stoke the flames of organizing further.

An open letter is best in situations with complex arguments. Letters give the space to write out an argument and essentially present a pitch to workers and leadership who might not immediately understand why the issue matters or its nuances. Letters provide space for long form arguments, and fit well in laying out a particular narrative without leaving room for ambiguity.

Open letters are also easy to share with the press. Sending an open letter to the press presents a very clear narrative that is less open to misinterpretation. Reporters can use the arguments made in the letter in their own stories, further contributing to your union's narrative.

How to write an open letter

Depending on your goals, there are a variety of tools available to create open letters. Typeform provides a sleek UI for an open letter, but isn't always user friendly for less tech-savvy users, and is more difficult for a group to use to write a letter collectively. If there is no intention to collect signatures, sharing a letter through Google Docs lets people read the letter in an easily accessible format while also supporting group writing.

Ultimately, the technology used to write the letter is less important than its contents and whether or not you want to support signatures. When writing an open letter, it's helpful to reiterate your why throughout the letter. Emphasize why you are writing this letter, and why it's important to you and your fellow workers. Share the reasons for your why and what led you to this point. The goal of the letter is to make a convincing argument and lay out your facts, but your facts will land harder when supported by the truth of your convictions.

Open letters are also most effective when they represent the voice of a collective. Rather than having just one person write the letter, writing a letter as a collective experience and ensuring multiple voices share their thoughts strengthens the arguments and the letter as a whole. Much like with unions as a whole, weaving more voices into the fabric only serves to strengthen the tapestry of the union as a whole.

One example of the power of an open letter comes from Apple-Together and its open letter on remote work. In June 2021, Apple leadership started notifying workers that the remote work policy it had had in place due to COVID was coming to an end, and workers would need to return to in-office work in the near future. For some Apple workers, the prospect of returning to the office was untenable. They organized in a Slack channel dedicated to remote work, and worked collectively to write an open letter. A group of a dozen organizers wrote an open letter, collecting stories from other workers throughout the company, and compiling their reasons for wanting to stay remote. They then sent this letter to all Apple workers via shared Slack channels, collecting signatures and asking for support.

The letter collected hundreds of signatures from workers throughout the company, sending a clear message that there was broad support for the reasons expressed in the open letter. In addition to signing the letter, workers flooded into the remote work Slack channel, hoping to find further resources on how to talk to their managers about working remotely, or to learn more about what actions were being taken to support continued remote work.

After gathering signatures, AppleTogether organizers sent the open letter to Apple leadership. A previous open letter had led to change within Apple, and so organizers were hopeful this letter would lead to a similar change in policy, or at least flexibility for those requesting continued remote work.

Instead, Apple leadership responded with a video that dismissed the concerns in the letter and reiterated the requirement that workers return to in-office work. The open letter and its signatures had not succeeded in its goal of convincing Apple leadership to change its policies.

However, the letter did demonstrate to workers throughout the company what leadership's stance on their working conditions was. For workers throughout the company, the dismissal of their concerns was a slap in the face. Workers continued to pour into the remote work Slack channel, citing their anger at leadership's video, and wanting to continue to put pressure on leadership. What had started as an open letter rapidly blossomed into a more structured, more determined organizing campaign. An open letter dismissed by leadership turned into what is now AppleTogether.

Though the letter did not succeed in its goals, it succeeded in accomplishing something more, namely, creating a worker movement fueled by a common "why." If Apple's leadership had been more flexible with that initial letter, it's entirely possible AppleTogether as it currently exists would not exist, as that common outrage would not have been fired up. However, leadership also would have been opening the door to more open letters and worker demands in the future, ultimately creating a workplace where workers had more power and sway over the course of their working conditions.

This is the power of an open letter. Picking a topic that a large number of workers support brings a company's response to worker action to the forefront. If a company chooses to acquiesce to requests in an open letter, this opens the door for further action in the future. If a company chooses to dismiss a letter, it fuels the fire of organizing by making it clear that the company is dismissive of workers' concerns. Open letters are a powerful way to gauge support, set tangible goals, and force a company's leadership to take a stand or risk further organizing.

Walkouts and Strikes

Walkouts and strikes are another set of actions that make very clear and visible statements about the seriousness of organizing and what actions workers are prepared to take. The two are very similar actions, with the primary difference being that a walkout has a set end time, and a strike generally does not.

How do walkouts and strikes work?

The goal of both walkouts and strikes is to make it clear that there is a particular issue that workers feel so strongly about, they are willing to stop work entirely to protest this issue. We previously discussed an example of B. Pagels-Minor and other Netflix organizers holding a walkout in protest of Netflix's airing of the Dave Chapelle special *The Closer*. In that case, Pagels-Minor and their fellow organizers believed Netflix's airing of the special represented a dehumanization of trans workers and creators, and a lack of willingness on the part of company leadership to engage with its trans workforce. Having tried other tactics to emphasize the importance of the issue, Netflix organizers turned to a work stoppage to emphasize how important addressing this issue was.[1]

Much like with an open letter, a walkout or strike should have a clear demand that the company should meet. Unlike with an open letter, this does not need to be supported with paragraph after paragraph of data. Instead, a walkout or strike is most effective when its demand is encapsulated in a few words. With the Netflix walkout, organizers presented a clear set of demands—improved representation of trans workers and creators—and walked out of their workplace to reinforce the seriousness of those demands.

How to organize a walkout or strike

Any action will take some degree of coordination. However, with a walkout or strike, that coordination may vary depending on the size of the company and the group intending to walkout. A small, local group is always easier to coordinate than a large or disparate one.

Planning a walkout or strike should include scheduling the event and its location, but also include whether there should be any further coordination. Decide in advance if there will be signs, chants, or matching colors. Everyone should also know why the strike or walkout is happening and be able to explain the reasons to curious passers-by or media. Unlike with open letters, any strike participant may be asked questions, and so preparing the group with answers ahead of time will help with controlling the narrative.

Walkouts and strikes have the added bonus of potentially being able to work in solidarity with other organizations supporting the same cause, depending on the reasons for the action. In the case of the

---

1. Interview with B. Pagels-Minor, 3 November 2022

Netflix walkout, Netflix workers worked in conjunction with several trans rights organizations to create a larger event than would have occurred than if it had just been Netflix workers. This larger event sent a clearer message to Netflix leadership, not only about Netflix workers' views, but about the larger community support for the workers and their cause.[2]

Potential consequences

However, as with any public-facing action, a walkout also has the potential of backfiring by creating the idea that the action is more about publicity and personal fame than inciting real change within a company. This is less so the case with strikes, as strikes require a majority of the workforce to participate if they are to be productive. With both, though, a high participation is required. If only a few workers participate, this may demonstrate a lack of support for the organizing movement, deflating enthusiasm for unionizing.

Strikes and walkouts are also inherently more dangerous than less visible or work-impacting activities. Because they involve very visible work stoppages, leadership may be more willing to act when a walkout or a strike is threatened. This, in turn, translates to a greater risk for organizers, though again, these are protected activities and retaliating against them is illegal.

The effectiveness of strikes and walkouts with coalition building and visibility cannot be overstated. A business relies on its workers to generate profits. Without workers, there are no profits, and so, strikes and walkouts can be effective tools to demonstrate to leadership how important an issue is and what the consequences are of not listening

---

2. Interview with B. Pagels-Minor, 3 November 2022

to workers. These actions also provide a more visible way for other organizations to express their support, through joining the walkout or expressing public support for a strike.

If you do choose to organize a strike or walkout, be sure to have sufficient participation and consider reaching out to others who support your reasons for organizing. This is easier with reasons that extend beyond particular workplace conditions, but never discount the power of coalition building when building a union. Connecting with other organizers makes everyone stronger.

Corporate and Legislative Structures

A third type of action is to use corporate and legislative structures to a movement's advantage. Shareholder proposals, appeals to the board of directors or funding sources, or pushing for legislative change require less coordinated action, but can be effective ways to force an issue to be addressed by a company. These channels are usually used by shareholders or those with a business interest rather than by workers. However, businesses are their workers. Using these pathways, while less traditional, are a viable path to change, especially for the tech industry, where compensation sometimes includes stock, and where venture capital funding can make or break a new company.

Legislation

To better understand why this route can be effective, let's re-examine a friend from a previous chapter—the Silenced No More Act in California. After their experience of discrimination at Pinterest and signing NDAs preventing them from discussing that experience, Aerica Shimizu Banks and Ifeoma Ozoma wanted to ensure that others did not have the same experience. As Banks put it, "You should have the right to your own story."[3] The pattern of companies systemically discriminating against workers of color and hiding that they did so through prohibitive NDAs meant that there was no way to hold companies to account or responsible for the harm they caused. Rather than staying silent, Banks and Ozoma chose instead to take legislative action to outlaw NDAs like the ones they had signed.

Banks used her previous policy experience to engage with lobbying groups and Senator Connie Leyva. Lobbying groups, while used by a wide variety of groups and interests, are most commonly associated with big business interests. Using these avenues co-opted the power that businesses usually use to regulate workers, and instead, turned it to workers regulating companies. Through significant lobbying and co-ordinating with related groups, Banks and Ozoma were successful in getting Silenced No More passed and forever changing the landscape of tech industry NDAs not only in California, but around the country.[4]

Shareholder Proposals

Shareholder proposals present a similar type of action that turns corporate avenues on their heads. Though activist shareholders are becoming more common, these types of initiatives usually come from very wealthy, external shareholders rather than workers themselves. However, for companies that provide compensation through stocks, there is nothing precluding workers themselves from filing sharehold-

---

3. Interview with Aerica Shimizu Banks, 18 October 2022

4. Interview with Aerica Shimizu Banks, 18 October 2022

er proposals that call attention to working conditions or other issues in the workplace.

This is one of the actions being pursued by AppleTogether. The 2022 Apple shareholder meeting saw multiple proposals brought forward by activist shareholders based on issues brought to light by the AppleToo movement.[5] While most were not successful, a shareholder proposal requesting a civil rights audit and another examining the impact of NDAs passed with shareholders, forcing Apple leadership to take action based on the shareholder votes. Inspired by these successes, organizers within AppleTogether began drafting their own shareholder proposals, centering on remote work and Apple's union busting of unionizing Apple stores. Though they didn't own thousands of AAPL shares, organizers realized that they could pool their shares and appoint a representative to be able to present proposals. In so doing, they would be forcing Apple leadership to address these issues directly, and potentially present their cases to all AAPL shareholders.[6]

Board of Directors

A board of directors holds significant sway over a company and its direction, but, more importantly, has a fiduciary responsibility to the company, requiring it to take actions to mitigate risks to a company. As B. Pagels-Minor points out, for small to medium companies, contacting the board about a particular issue that could turn into a lawsuit or similar legal action can be a quick way to see change. If the board

---

5. https://www.theverge.com/2022/3/4/22962097/apple-nda-harassment-civil-rights-shareholder-meeting-tim-cook

6. Interview with Megan Mohr, 18 October 2022

is informed about an issue and chooses not to take action, this also furthers any legal argument that might later come up.[7]

Funding sources

Similarly, for start-ups receiving funding from venture capital firms or similar sources, approaching these funding sources with issues may be a way to bring attention to an issue. Funding is provided with the hope of a return on an investment, and being made aware of a threat to that potential return on investment can be a powerful motivator for a fund to reach out to a company about its behavior. This is also an action any individual can take. Be plausible and stick to the facts, and provide documentation, but making a board member or a venture capital firm aware of what's actually going on at a company can be a powerful way to spur change from the top down.[8]

One unique element of the tech industry is its entrepreneurial culture. It's this same entrepreneurial culture that can be weaponized into a powerful tool of organizing. What is more inaccessible in industries is more accessible in tech. Using these alternate forms of organizing and action can still achieve impressive results.

Media Involvement

The media is a double-edged sword. The decision to use it is one that must always be made with the knowledge that there are consequences, positive and negative, but strong ones nonetheless.

---

7. Interview with B. Pagels-Minor, 3 November 2022

8. Interview with B. Pagels-Minor, 3 November 2022

Depending on the company you're in, media involvement may not be a choice. Large, multinational companies tend to attract attention, and reporters will likely be interested in speaking with you, whether you're interested in publicizing your union or not. It's important to decide to what extent you'll engage with the media and what you intend to accomplish through that engagement.

Pros and Cons

The media fundamentally exists as a way to engage with power, either by holding it to account or reinforcing its beliefs, depending on the goals of a particular publication or even a particular journalists. It provides a powerful way to gain an audience and to spread a message more widely than is possible on one's own. Some journalists have come to be seen as allies of the tech labor movement for their tenacity in reporting on organizing and unions in the industry.

This publicity, however, comes at a cost. As with the discussion in a previous chapter on preparing to be an organizer, once a story reaches the media, it ceases to be in the control of those whom the story is about. A union might be portrayed in ways its creators could not have predicted, both negatively and positively. That portrayal creates a feedback loop, both for internal and external audiences. How fellow workers view a union may come to be seen less through the lens of the conversations organizers are having with them, and more through the lens of the media reporting on the union.

It's also possible there is no attention whatsoever, potentially deflating some of the enthusiasm for organizing. The outcome of reaching out to the press is ultimately unpredictable, though a few factors may hold true.

Potential consequences

In general, the press is a more useful tool in larger companies, where the sheer size of the company makes it prohibitively difficult to speak to a meaningfully large number of colleagues about unionizing. The press can draw attention to actions that are being taken and the fact that there is a unionization effort, reaching more people and granting a legitimacy that might not otherwise have been possible if communication happened on any individual basis. This is especially true of companies like Google and Apple, where the press has and continues to play a critical role in informing large swaths of the company about worker actions in sections of the company they might not have even known existed.

For smaller companies, the press can potentially cause backlash. Unless a company has already been in the news significantly, the press doesn't necessarily reach workers in a more meaningful way than a conversation would. Instead, press attention can create the idea that organizers are less interested in the company and their coworkers' wellbeing, and more interested in the publicity and fame that can potentially come with being an organizer.

One example of how press involvement can shape a movement comes from Kickstarter. Kickstarter had two major instances of press involvement, each of which shifted the conversation in a different way. Because of how small and local the company was, Kickstarter's OC made the decision to keep its conversations and activities internal. This allowed them to keep their activities out of the public eye, and ensure conversations were happening worker to worker, rather than being passed through the lens of press attention. However, shortly after sending an e-mail to workers about the unionization effort and its motivations, this e-mail was leaked to the press, who promptly reported on Kickstarter's unionization efforts.[9]

For some who had been unaware of the union, this was an exciting moment, and they rushed to reach out to the contacts listed in the e-mail to show their support and willingness to join the union. However, for others, the e-mail being reported on in the press was a sign of bad faith on the part of the union. Rather than choosing to keep internal conversations internal, some in the company saw the media attention as attention-seeking behavior and a sign that union organizers were acting in bad faith.[10]

The decision to have the e-mail go to the press was not a decision the OC made. However, once in the press, the narrative about who the union was and why they were organizing was removed from their hands, and instead, became seen through the lens of the press attention. For Kickstarter leadership, this presented an opportunity to rebut the pro-union arguments through the release of anti-union talking points. These talking points successfully convinced some workers within the company that the union was mainly "troublemakers" who were "using the press to 'pressure' workers into voting or in retaliation for anti union sentiment." The narrative and framing of worker actions as being by workers, for workers was lost when they lost control of the narrative, being replaced instead by others' interpretations of their actions. The conversation, rather than being between workers, instead became between some workers and the world. Ultimately,

---

9. Interview with Clarissa Redwine, 8 November 2022

10. Interview with Clarissa Redwine, 8 November 2022

                    JANNEKE PARRISH

this initial leak became seen as doing more harm than good for their organizing.[11]

However, the Kickstarter union also had a second instance of press involvement, one that ultimately did do more good than harm. In response to unionization efforts, in September 2019, Kickstarter began firing organizers, ostensibly for performance-related issues. One at a time, Kickstarter organizers were fired, beginning with Clarissa Redwine, and followed by Taylor Moore. Each was offered a severance agreement in exchange for a non-disparagement agreement. Rather than accept, Redwine and Moore tweeted publicly about what was happening at Kickstarter, letting the media know that Kickstarter was retaliating against organizers.[12]

This decision had an immediate impact. The press began reporting on Kickstarter's actions, subjecting their actions to scrutiny and bringing wide publicity to their union busting. This, in turn, dramatically shifted the union busting at Kickstarter. Rather than summarily firing another organizer, as they had done with Redwine and Moore, Kickstarter leadership instead turned their meeting with a third organizer into a negotiation, giving the organization movement significant leverage. Continued media attention on Kickstarter also potentially prevented more firings, as the company found itself under significant scrutiny.[13]

The decision to go public about the firings was also not without backlash. For those within the company who believed the initial leak

---

11. Interview with Clarissa Redwine, 8 November 2022

12. https://techworkerhandbook.org/stories/clarissa-redwine/

13. Interview with Clarissa Redwine, 8 November 2022

had been an attention-seeking gesture, going public with news about the firings did nothing to change that perception. The belief became that the fired organizers in some way deserved what had happened.

However, for others, seeing their coworkers get fired and understanding the context in which it was happening proved to be a galvanizing moment. Workers realized what leadership was doing, and that it did not have their best interests at heart. To a certain degree, the media attention helped the union gain strength and support.

The decision to blow the whistle about the firings was a strategic one rather than one done outside the control of the union. This fundamentally shifted how the outcome could play out. Because organizers chose what to share and when to share it, they had more control over the narrative and how it could shape the outcome. Though Redwine and Moore's hands were partly forced due to the circumstances of their firings and the imminentness of another organizer's firing, their decision to share what was happening at Kickstarter was still their own. Because of that control over the narrative, they were able to leverage newfound public support for the benefit of the union.[14]

Public support is fickle, and relying on it is unwise. Stories that make headlines can be quickly forgotten, and the public can choose to create its own narratives around what they read. Though Kickstarter benefitted in the short term from media attention, it is unclear if it benefitted in the long term from the potential workplace schisms that arose from the decision to share what was happening within Kickstarter with the press.

Ironically, though it's unclear how media attention impacted Kickstarter's union, media attention did benefit the labor movement in tech as a whole. With Kickstarter's decision to unionize and the wide-

---

14. Interview with Clarissa Redwine, 8 November 2022

spread publicity surrounding it, other companies used their example as an inspiration to pursue their own unionization efforts. Code for America organizers specifically cited Kickstarter's example when making the decision to unionize and pitching it to their fellow workers.[15] An individual movement might suffer from press attention, but the labor movement as a whole benefits from knowing when others succeed, or at least when pro-union thoughts and organizers aren't on their own.

Before engaging with the media, consider what outcome you are hoping to achieve. If you work in a large company and need an effective way to reach many people at once, the media can be an effective tool to help achieve that. Similarly, if leadership is taking actions that threaten your union, and calling attention to those actions can help stop them, the media may be a useful tool. However, media attention for its own sake is not always a good thing.

What is your goal?

Before engaging with the press, consider what the purpose is, and carefully consider the potential consequences. The press is best used when dealing with an urgent action, or in the face of union busting that can't otherwise be stopped. Taking control of the narrative and ensuring that the story being told is one that needs to be told to drive accountability is the best of the press.

However, any use of the press will always come with backlash. Even in cases of urgency, be cautious and aware that having internal issues broadcast to the world will always cause the union to lose at least some degree of internal support. Weigh the pros and cons carefully before

---

15. Interview with Ben Calegari, 11 November 2022

reaching out publicly, and be prepared to explain the decision to go public internally.

Social Media

Similarly, social media provides a powerful tool for communication, but comes with the same drawbacks of losing internal support. As with traditional media, think carefully about what purpose social media should serve.

What is your goal?

One use is in conjunction with traditional media. A union using its social media presence to amplify stories written about it can help elevate those stories and create a broader conversation about organizing throughout the tech industry. Social media also provides a handy way for workers who might not otherwise know who to reach out to a platform where they're guaranteed to be able to speak to an organizer anonymously. Social media also provides a platform for solidarity with other unions and creating connections that can help support organizers across different companies in their common goals to unionize.

Who benefits the most?

As with traditional media, social media is best used with large companies who otherwise can't reach everyone. A social media presence provides a hub for information and outreach, while also amplifying issues company-wide. A smaller company is better off engaging in conversations and word of mouth, rather than making the union's existence more public.

Once a union gains traction and goes public, there will always be press outreach. It is always completely acceptable to decline to speak to the press and maintain that communications are internal only. It is also always okay to speak to the press on background or under the condition of anonymity. All respectable journalists will respect your wish on how public you want to be.

What action should I take?

Which action to take is largely dependent on your particular circumstances. However, the group should buy in to the action and its intended outcome. Work together to set up a plan and a strategy, and incorporate elements of the action throughout. Taking action for its own sake is not sustainable. Rather, actions play a useful role in propelling a movement forward, keeping members motivated, and letting fellow workers know what their power can achieve.

It's not always possible to predict what the outcome of an action will be. However, through careful planning and control of the narrative, it's possible to make an action as effective as possible.

8. Recognition, Elections, and Contracts

The process of building a union is an arduous one. Between pitching the idea to coworkers, facing down union busting, and making strategic decisions about what actions to take, why, and when, there is an almost endless array of options ahead of any organizer, and the consequences of choosing the wrong thing can have a dramatic outcome.

One of the most consequential decisions, though, is the decision of when and how to approach the company for recognition. This is the point where quiet organizing becomes loud. It's where other workers can see how much power the union effort actually has. Potentially, it's also the first time a company learns there is a union drive. It has to be good.

The Recognition Process

Getting official recognition as a union begins and ends with the NLRB. The NLRB provides an overview of the entire process on its website, but here is a brief overview of the recognition process:

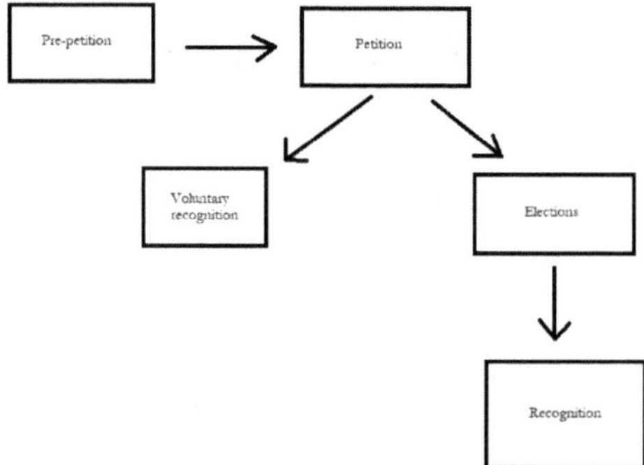

Fig. 8.1: The NLRB Recognition Process

Let's review each step in turn.

Pre-petition Steps

Before involving the NLRB, there must sufficient support among members of the bargaining unit. Understanding who comprises a bargaining unit is important for the upcoming recognition. For the NLRB, a bargaining unit can be understood to be workers working for the same employer in a non-management role who form a community of interest.[1] A community of interest has further criteria, some of which include similar work, similar working conditions, regular

---

1. https://guide.unitworkers.com/whats-a-bargaining-unit/

contact with one another, similar wages, or common supervision. The actual determination of whether or not a given bargaining unit is done by the NLRB.[2] In general, a whole-employer union is considered a bargaining unit. If there are any concerns about whether or not your union is a valid bargaining unit, it's best to discuss those concerns with a labor attorney, or with the union you are working with, if you are working with a larger union.

In order to prove there is sufficient support for a union, organizers need to conduct a card check. This is the process of reaching out to union members and having them more formally indicate their support for the union by signing a union authorization card. This can be done either in print or digitally, depending on the specifics of the union and the workplace.[3] For larger workplaces or remote ones, sharing the card digitally might make more sense than trying to collect physical versions.

With both cases, there are some fields that are required by the NLRB. If you're working with a national union, they generally have a template that contains all the fields the NLRB needs. However, if you're an independent union, you would need to build your own card. Because the purpose of the card is to confirm that there is support for the union, it must contain the following fields:

- Full name

- E-mail

---

2. http://labored.missouri.edu/documents/2005-07.pdf

3. https://www.nlrb.gov/about-nlrb/rights-we-protect/the-law/e mployees/your-right-to-form-a-union

- Phone number

- Employer

- Signature

- Date of signature

It must also contain an explicit statement that the signatory is giving collective bargaining rights to the union. It can also be helpful to include the following:

- Address

- Employer's address

- Job title

- Hire date

- Type of work performed

- Shift or work hours

- Type of employment (full-time, part-time, etc.)

- Pay range

- Whether the worker would like to be part of the OC

These cards are only seen by the union and the NLRB, so while the first set of fields are needed for the NLRB, the second set are extremely helpful for the union to better understand conditions and composition of the union.

A union authorization card is not itself a binding agreement to be bound by a union. A worker has the right to request their card back at any point, nor does a card compel them to vote in favor of the union. Rather, the card's purpose is to show the NLRB that there is support for a union.

This ability to retract an authorization card also means that the card check can be subject to particularly heavy union busting. Before any union election can take place, a union must have cards from at least 30% of the bargaining unit. If it can reach 50% plus one, union representatives can reach out to the employer directly, requesting voluntary recognition.

However, the power of the card check means there is a strong disincentive for employers to allow it to happen. Once an employer is aware of or even suspects a card check is happening, it is not uncommon for employers to issue no soliciting policies meant to target union organizers, making it more difficult to collect physical cards. The company may also lie about what signing a card grants to a union, or mislead workers about how the card check is going.[4] If it's possible to keep card collection discreet, the best strategy is for a company to be unaware it's happening. However, if the employer does find out and begins union busting, organizers should be prepared with both proactive inoculation against lies, and with reactive responses to what management is saying.

It can also be helpful to consider a digital route. Creating a digital card can be as simple as a Google form, though it may be helpful to create something more secure to protect signatories' confidentiality. A link to the digital card can be sent out over any platform, and is just as legally valid as a physical card. This lack of physicality also makes the

---

4. https://www.jwj.org/wp-content/uploads/2014/03/Logan-Consultants.pdf

presence of a card check harder to detect, providing an extra layer of security.[5]

Those who sign e-cards still have the same rights as physical signatories, namely, the right to withdraw their card. However, if the digital campaign is quiet, there may be less union busting, and thus, fewer workers reaching out to withdraw their cards.

Though a union only needs 30% of workers to sign a union authorization card to move forward with an NLRB petition, successful card checks will need significantly more support. Generally, unions do not go public with their organizing at 30% or even 50%. Rather, because of the effect union busting on union membership, most unions prefer to go public with 60-70% support, depending on the size of the bargaining unit. This way, even if members are dissuaded from joining due to union busting, the campaign as a whole isn't lost.

Once you have enough people to go public, it's time to announce your union! Making sure to announce at an appropriate time is also critical for maintaining morale within the union. One example of the devastating impact a premature announcement can have comes from an Apple store in St. Louis. Workers in St. Louis had been working with the national union, the International Association of Machinists and Aerospace Workers (IAM), to build a union for their store. Though organizing had been successful, IAM submitted union authorization cards to the NLRB before the store's OC believed they

---

5. https://ogletree.com/insights/click-here-to-organize-nlrb-now -accepts-e-signatures-on-authorization-cards/

were ready, and against the OC's wishes. In response, 79% of the workers asked that their petition be withdrawn.[6]

The choice to move forward prematurely cost the St. Louis union dearly. What had been a viable unionization campaign lost the faith and trust of its members when IAM submitted a petition against their wishes. Instead of gaining representation, the store became divided and lost faith in what they had been organizing towards.

Union building is inherently an act of trust: trusting others with stories, trusting fellow workers to stand in solidarity, and ultimately, trusting that a union will indeed represent everyone's best interests. A card check is one of the major steps that helps show how much trust has been built, and how much still needs to be done. When over a majority of workers are willing to trust in the union they've built, and are willing to sign an authorization card, it's a sign that the union is ready. It's time to move towards recognition.

Petition

Once your union has sufficient support, it's time to file a petition with the NLRB. The NLRB maintains a list of forms on its website, and I have included a link to this list in the Resources section. A first-time union uses form NLRB-502 (RC). A link to this form is included in the resources section of this book.

Much like with other NLRB forms, this form is fairly straightforward. If you are working with a larger union, they will often file this

---

6. https://9to5mac.com/2022/12/05/st-louis-staff-explain-givin
g-up-unionization/

on your union's behalf. If you are an independent union, the NLRB provides support in filling out the form, if needed.

Recognition

Recognition is tough. Not only is it the culmination of months of work and the emotional investment of so many conversations, it's the ultimate moment of truth, a determination of whether or not a movement can withstand the tests before it. It's also a moment of truth in understanding how a company will truly respond. Even for campaigns that have faced union busting, once the union has its majority, there is always the option for the company to voluntarily recognize the union. There is a tension in wondering—and hoping—they will, and potentially, the disappointment when they don't.

Voluntary recognition

It is entirely possible that a company will choose to voluntarily recognize a union, though this is rare. Voluntary recognition generally occurs in very small companies, or in cases where a company worries what might happen to its reputation if it does not voluntarily recognize a union.

One example of a voluntary recognition comes from Vodeo Workers United. Formed in 2021, Vodeo Workers United was a union for workers at Vodeo Games. Similar to Code for America, these workers chose to unionize, not because of any particular inciting circumstance within their workplace, but partly as an act of solidarity with other game unions, such as United Paizo Workers. Rather than making large changes, their union sought to ensure that many of the perks that had enjoyed would continue to exist into the future.[7]

Vodeo Games had thirteen workers working remotely across the United States and Canada.[8] This small number of workers meant both that organizing was easier—in that there were fewer conversations that needed to be had—but also that the opportunity for the union to fail was greater. If more than a handful of workers had objected, there would have been no hope of the union succeeding. However, the union chose to focus on maintaining existing benefits and having a seat at the table rather than being antagonistic. It's possible this approach helped it succeed and maintain the unity it needed to have a majority.

Vodeo Games ultimately chose to recognize the union voluntarily rather than going to an election. Though the company itself is now defunct, the achievement of the workers in organizing a fully remote, contractor-inclusive union still stands.

Another example of a voluntary recognition comes from Code for America. A significantly larger company, CfA's union was also recognized voluntarily, albeit with significant hesitation and hurdles.

When organizers asked for voluntary recognition from leadership, CfA's initial response was to delay the timeline for recognition. A process that should have taken a week instead stretched into months, with leadership raising objections about the union's composition and claiming to need the time to understand what a power-sharing

---

7. https://www.polygon.com/22834924/vodeo-games-first-video
-game-union-north-america-code-cwa

8. https://www.polygon.com/22834924/vodeo-games-first-vide
o-game-union-north-america-code-cwa

arrangement could look like. For organizers, these delays looked less like good faith attempts to understand what a CfA union would look like, and more like a lack of engagement with the process.[9]

However, the true pressure to recognize the union ultimately came from CfA's own missteps. CfA leadership hired a union busting firm, Jackson Lewis, to advise on how best to respond to the union. CfA, however, existed in a sphere of highly politically active workers and donors, many of whom did not look kindly on attempts to curtail workers' rights through union busting. Hiring Jackson Lewis increased the public pressure on CfA to recognize the union voluntarily, especially from its donors. When union organizers reached out to the NLRB to organize an election, CfA chose instead to voluntarily recognize the union. The combination of relentlessness from union organizers and public pressure from their donors led Code for America to recognize its workers' rights to organize.[10] In this case, the power of these workers' voices on its own was enough to persuade CfA to recognize the union.

Both of these cases are rare examples of voluntary recognition, and both have unique circumstances associated with them. For Vodeo, it's likely the combination of the motivation for the union, the company's own financial situation, and the size of the company factored heavily into the decision not to hold an election. For Code for America, public perception and the need to maintain a certain public image led to a voluntary recognition.

---

9. Interview with Ben Calegari, 11 November 2022

10. Interview with Ben Calegari, 11 November 2022

Recognition through Elections

More commonly, a company will refuse to voluntarily recognize a union. Instead, the NLRB will organize an election where eligible workers will be asked to vote on whether or not they wish to form a union.

If a company does not voluntarily recognize the union, the NLRB follows the procedures for an election.[11] It can be a few weeks between when the NLRB decides there will be an election to when the election takes place. Throughout that time, companies can file objections, ask for reviews, or generally place hurdles in the way, prolonging the amount of time it will take before the election actually takes place. For a union, this can be one of the most dangerous parts of the campaign. It is at this point that the campaign is public, and the company will be doing all it can to union bust. Though union busting is illegal, if a company worries they might lose the election, it is at this point that they will crack down on organizers using many of the techniques discussed in the earlier chapter on union busting.[12]

11.

https://www.employer.gov/EmploymentIssues/Union-and-pro tected-concerted-activity/What-rules-govern-how-I-interact-wit h-union-representatives/

12. https://www.jwj.org/wp-content/uploads/2014/03/Logan -Consultants.pdf

Preparing for elections

For organizers, being aware of and responding quickly to any objections and union busting is critical. Continuing to show solidarity among workers helps mitigate the impact of the union busting that will take place at this point. Similarly, making the NLRB aware of illegal union busting the company may be doing also helps the NLRB ensure the election is as fair as possible. If the NLRB determines that an election was not fair, it's possible there may be a new election entirely, though this is rare.

What does an election need?

Elections, much like the card check, rely on a majority plus one of participants to vote for a union. However, unlike card checks, the number is not based on the number of workers in the bargaining unit, but rather, based on the number of voters who participate in the election. This means that, even if a bargaining unit has a hundred people in it, if just one person actually votes, it is that person who decides whether or not there will be a union.[13] Because of this, getting out the vote is just as critical as persuading others on how to vote.

Because of this, it can be helpful to think of a union election campaign as not dissimilar to a political campaign. It's helpful to build hype and to establish just how much support the union has, as well as emphasize the importance of voting. One common technique to get out the vote is to build a "I'm voting yes" campaign and provide some sort of sign of solidarity to show clear support for the union.

---

13. https://www.polygon.com/23485977/video-game-unions-guide-explainer

Solidarity campaigns

For workers in the Oklahoma City Apple Store, this show of solidarity came in the form of red wristbands. Workers planning to vote in favor of the union wore red wristbands to express their support and provide a visual reminder to one another that none of them were alone. This also showed workers on the fence about a union how many of their fellow workers were in support, helping them lean towards voting yes.[14]

Other Apple stores have included testimonials from workers about why they are voting yes as part of their public social media campaigns. These testimonials show memoji versions of workers with a small blurb, putting a human face and voice to each "yes" vote. Combined with excitement about voting yes to a union, these types of campaigns are effective ways to not only build hype, but potentially maintain public interest in the case of campaigns that are facing union busting.

Once again, though, it is important not to forget that it is conversations that build the bedrock of unions. Continually checking in with members and making sure as many people as possible are planning to vote yes remains important, as does reassuring those who may have doubts, or may be struggling from union busting.

Outreach

Companies are legally required to provide organizers with a list of all workers who are eligible to vote in the upcoming election, including

---

14. Interview with Michael Forsythe, 26 September 2022

their address, and potentially phone number and e-mail address.[15] Though they are legally required to provide this, some may intentionally provide the most out-of-date or incomplete information they can in an attempt to stymie further organizing.[16] As a result, the union should try to build its own contact list as much as possible, supplementing it with the information provided by the company.

Once the election date is set, it's helpful to set a plan for contacting everyone on the list. For in-person workplaces, this can again be setting up conversations or meet-ups, though a company may ban these sorts of meetings during work hours or in work spaces. Instead, it can again be helpful to draw on techniques from political campaigns, such as textbanking or phone banking.

Text and phone banking are two variations on the same idea—using a list of phone numbers to either text or call a large list of workers. This can be especially effective for middle-sized companies, as the list of workers can be prohibitively large for in-person contacts, and especially effective for remote companies.[17] Though no one likes to receive spam texts or calls, these are still effective ways for a small group of people to make a human connection efficiently. These methods can also be very cheap, and numerous softwares exist that streamline the process.

---

15. https://www.nlrb.gov/news-publications/publications/fact-sheets/nlrb-representation-case-procedures-fact-sheet

16. https://www.jwj.org/wp-content/uploads/2014/03/Logan-Consultants.pdf

17. Interview with Ben Calegari, 11 November 2022

Continuing to make contact and reinforce that yes vote is also important. Though campaigning less than 24 hours before the vote is not allowed, continuing to check in before that point helps reassure workers that they are not alone, and that voting yes is still the right decision. This also presents an opportunity for them to ask any final questions they have. Whether that contact is through conversations, phone banking, or textbanking, keep in contact with fellow workers, and ensure that no one feels left out or unsure.

What to do if you lose the majority

It may be the case that, over the course of these conversations, it becomes clear the majority has slipped away, or that, for whatever reason, the election may not winnable. It is possible to cancel an election at any point, and in some cases, it can be helpful to do so. If an election fails to win a majority, while the union process is not forever halted, it can be years before the union is able to file for another election. However, if a petition is withdrawn, there is instead a six month wait before being able to file again. It can be strategically helpful to withdraw the petition and instead refile after six months. However, this also comes with significant risk. The company is aware that there is a unionizing campaign, and now knows what steps are effective when it comes to union busting. A refiled petition is unlikely to succeed without drastic changes in the workplace.

Elections

Election day is here! Elections are held by the NLRB, and, unlike with card checks, the election itself takes place with physical ballots, either at a ballot box, or through mail. For in-person workplaces, this will most likely be a ballot box, while remote or hybrid workplaces will likely be through the mail. Encouraging people to vote through reminders of the importance of voting, the repetition of the election date, and making it possible for as many people as possible to get to the ballot box as possible is vital. The outcome is not dependent on eligible voters, but on the number of actual voters. The more voters in favor of unionizing who vote, the better the odds will be.

The ballots are anonymous, though who votes and doesn't vote is tracked. The final NLRB outcome will include not only the actual outcome of the vote, but also how many of the eligible workers actually voted. The actual counting is done live, with both the employer and the union welcome to attend. There, the votes are individually counted, with the NLRB verifying that each vote is valid.[18] Months of organizing reach their zenith in this moment, waiting for the final tally. At the end of the session, it's clear whether the vote was successful, and whether there will be a union.

Objections

After the vote and the tallies, both parties still have the opportunity to raise any objections. The NLRB will hear objections to the outcome for seven days after the final vote. For the company, this can be a further opportunity to union bust by filing objection after objection in the hopes that one will stick and the election will need to be redo

---

18. https://guide.unitworkers.com/making-it-official-union-electi on-certification/

ne.[19] For organizers who have lost an election, this period provides an opportunity to present any union busting that may have contributed to the lost election, and potentially receive a do-over.[20] However, if there are no objections, or no objections are found to have merit, the outcome stands. There either is a union, or there is not a union. The organizers have either won, or they have not.

Elections are emotionally exhausting. All the work that went into building a campaign before going public now kicks into high gear, but with the ever-looming specter of union busting and the clear presence of an employer who is definitely aware of the union effort. Throughout the book, we have discussed the importance of self-care; at no point is that more important than during an election campaign. Keeping members of the union safe and healthy is vital, and standing in solidarity, regardless of the company's actions keeps everyone safe.

Elections are winnable. They are difficult, and they require work, but to even get to this point, organizers will have already proven how capable and dedicated they are. Elections aren't the easy part, but they are the part that publicly reaffirms workers' power. They're a chance to prove what workers can do, and to finally make a union a reality.

Negotiation and Contracts

If you've gotten this far, the hard part of unionizing is over. You've won your election. You have a union. It's okay to take a moment and

---

19. https://www.jwj.org/wp-content/uploads/2014/03/Logan-C onsultants.pdf

20. https://guide.unitworkers.com/making-it-official-union-electi on-certification/

just feel relief. Congratulate yourself on everything you've done. You rallied your fellow workers. You made your pitch. You overcame union busting and convinced others to take a stand for their rights and their futures.

It's not over yet.

Once an election is finished, the NLRB will verify everything is correct. If it is, the NLRB will certify the election, and the union becomes the collective bargaining representative. The union then elects a bargaining committee, comprising a diverse group of workers who represent the broad range of interests in the company.[21] Through having a diverse group of negotiators, the union ensures that the upcoming union contract will be as representative and inclusive of all workers' needs as possible.

Not every union needs a contract. For some unions, it's enough to have the union and its power to take protected, collective action. There is still significant power just in being able to act collectively and ensure that workers' voices are heard. However, a contract is the only binding way to ensure a company will adhere to a union's demands, and so many unions pursue a contract.[22]

Negotiations

The company has an obligation to negotiate in good faith with the union, and will face an unfair labor practice charge if they do not

---

21. https://www.polygon.com/23485977/video-game-unions-gui
de-explainer

22. https://www.polygon.com/23485977/video-game-unions-gui
de-explainer

do so.[23] However, just because the law establishes what a company's behavior should be doesn't mean that reflects what the behavior will be in reality. Though the union is in place and has the legal right and responsibility to engage with the company on behalf of the bargaining unit, companies may still try to stymie a union at every turn.

An example of how this continued union busting manifests comes from Code from America. After voluntarily recognizing the CfA union, workers elected a bargaining committee who would engage with CfA and represent the group. This bargaining committee worked with the union membership as a whole to create a list of what they wanted. The committee and the company worked together to schedule regular negotiation meetings where they would discuss what workers wanted, and how both sides could come to an agreement. Both sides presented themselves as acting in good faith when negotiations began in February 2022.[24]

However, as negotiations continued, the bargaining committee began to believe leadership was not acting in good faith. Rather than discussing the items that organizers wanted to see in a contract, CfA leadership instead focusing on miniscule details and non-economic elements, such as the number of stewards involved in negotiations. Leadership was slow to respond, delaying negotiations further under the guise of needing a better understanding, or doing more research. During negotiations, leadership also moved organizers to roles that were ineligible to be part of the union, or made incorrect statements about eligibility, further negating the power of the union.

---

23. https://guide.unitworkers.com/making-it-official-union-election-certification/

24. Interview with Ben Calegari, 11 November 2022

For committee member Ben Calegari, though it wasn't overt that CfA leadership wasn't acting in good faith, it was clear that they were more subtly union busting. After nine months of negotiating, the bargaining committee wasn't any closer to a contract than it had been at the start of negotiations, and members of the union were beginning to lose faith.[25]

The loss of faith in the union is one of the key drivers for why companies continue union busting during the negotiation stage. Once a union is in place, it is not impossible to remove. Similar to a union certification election, if enough workers lose faith in a union, they can petition for a de-certification election and vote on whether to remove the union from its position. For companies that have lost an election and now face a union, making the union seem powerless and ineffectual provides fuel to the potential fire of a de-certification election. Continuing to union bust by not negotiating in good faith can potentially lead to that de-certification and the removal of a union they did not want.[26]

Unions who are facing a stalled negotiation process have a few options to reassure their members that they are acting to the best of their ability, and, more importantly, convince management to make a deal with them. Strikes and other solidarity actions such as those discussed in the chapter on actions provide a powerful way to make a statement about worker power and the power of the union. Though these still carry the same risk with them, they can be effective negotiating tools.

---

25. Interview with Ben Calegari, 11 November 2022

26. https://www.jwj.org/wp-content/uploads/2014/03/Logan-Consultants.pdf

However, Calegari and his fellow committee members found an alternate method. Negotiating sessions are open to all, though generally only attended by the bargaining committee. Calegari and his fellow negotiators invited union members to sit in on the sessions to better understand how the company was behaving and how they were acting in bad faith. For Calegari, the negotiating process was eye-opening, with him saying "I didn't see why we needed a union until I saw how they reacted to something common sense."[27]

Calegari has also been reminded of the strategy the union used to gain recognition in the first place. As a non-profit dependent on donations and maintaining a positive public image, the potential of going public with the company's bad faith negotiation has a potentially large impact. The actions that worked to create the union can also be used to create a contract, if needed.[28]

Even with these tactics, though, it is important to keep in mind that negotiation is exactly that—a negotiation. Much as the company will not get everything it wants, the union also will not get everything it wants. That knowledge should never be a barrier to acting in good faith. As long as the union effectively represents the desires of the workers it represents, it can be considered successful.

Contracts

Once management and the bargaining committee agree on a contract, the contract then goes back to the members of the union to ratify. This is the last chance for everyone to have a say in the contract and collec-

27. Interview with Ben Calegari, 11 November 2022

28. Interview with Ben Calegari, 11 November 2022

tively agree on whether or not it is acceptable. This is finally an election that doesn't require campaigning or get out the vote drives—members of the union vote, and it is the outcome of that election that decides whether or not there is a contract.[29]

The work of the union doesn't end with a contract. A union is, first and foremost, a representative of the workers and a liaison between workers and management, ensuring workers' rights are protected, and management is abiding by the terms of the contract it has signed. It must still listen to workers, take action when needed, and be there to support and organize solidarity. However, with a contract in place, the hardest part is over. The next steps are maintenance and recognizing the power that workers acting in unison have to improved all of their lives.

---

29. https://www.polygon.com/23485977/video-game-unions-gui
de-explainer

What will your voice achieve?

Your voice has power.

There are innumerable barriers trying to prevent your voice from being heard. From organized union busting to systemic structures to the very nature of fear and consequences, the number of barriers is seemingly insurmountable.

And yet.

And yet, in case after case, unions succeed. The NLRB lists out all the recent union elections and their outcomes, and in case after case, workplace after workplace, workers are winning. Despite the barriers, despite the array of forces levied against them, workers are succeeding in making their voices heard. They are making themselves part of the decision-making framework of their workplaces. They are forging their workplaces into what they would like them to be.

You are doing that. You, the reader, are a worker too, and you, the reader, are a part of this movement too.

None of us believes we could be the one to do it. Each of us has, to some extent, internalized the barriers, or spent so long hearing that we can't that when we are finally told we can, it seems almost impossible to believe. That spark of organizing, that ability to forge something independent of and greater than any one of us, that lies in each of our hearts. It's just waiting for the right fan to send it swirling into an inferno.

In talking to your fellow workers, you'll find their sparks. Each of us has a reason for doing what we're doing, for pressing on through the day-to-day, and for dreaming of what could be. We all have a dream, and we all have something we want to see.

For Steven, from AppleTogether, there is more to organizing than the rewards. As he puts it: "A company is a collection of people, especially when so much of it is intellectual in nature. If you're not treating those people with respect—whoever they are, whatever their role—what are you even doing?" He and his fellow workers have organized in one of the largest companies in the world, seeing their fellow organizers get fired. They've still managed to win meaningful change for themselves and their fellow workers.

For Laurel, from AppleTogether, organizing is how change is enabled. As she puts it: "We're not just here to vent. We're here to do something."

For contract workers like Robert and workers in Malaysia, unions have the ability to change not only workspaces, but lives. For Robert, having a union would mean "I could look at the work I was doing and value the work I was doing and the impact I was having, rather than the work of whoever was sitting in this spot, and that has an effect on how I view myself." For workers in Malaysia, a union presents the opportunity to change. Currently, "You're not allowed to follow your dreams because of what you are." A union could change their world as much as it could change their American counterparts'.

For Megan Mohr, who, in 2022, inspired by the activism occurring in the industry and the solidarity from her fellow workers, came forward with her experience of dealing with sexual assault at Apple. "It doesn't seem scary in this moment," she said. "I've never regretted speaking up, and I have definitely regretted not speaking up."

The action of unionizing makes the entire industry better. For Jessica, from Activision-Blizzard, "The beacon of light that shone on the industry kind of helped...with everyone collectively making the industry better."

But the thought that hangs above all, the image of what unionizing can be for the people inside it comes from Michael, from the Penn Square Apple Store in Oklahoma City. For him, "[It's] not my journey I'm trying to change. I want this to change my wife's work life. I hope this creates enough change to offer maternity leave. It's what she deserves." He and his fellow workers have organized in one of the largest companies in the world, fighting union busting so severe, the NLRB has called it illegal. They won anyway.

It is in using our voices that we can change the world. It is in speaking in unison that we build something better. It is in listening that we hear the change we want to bring about echoed back through a thousand throats.

Your voice has power. It's time to use it.

Acknowledgements

Thank you to everyone who believed in this book and in me to write it. Thank you to Sharina Wunderink for your patient editing, and to Grace Keller Scotch for the cover art.

Thank you as well to everyone who gave their time, experiences, and expertise. Thank you to Michael Forsythe, Laurel Degutis, Steven McGrath, Megan Mohr, and everyone at AppleTogether. Thank you to Jessica Gonzalez, Laurence Berland, Aerica Shimizu Banks, Ben Calegari, Clarissa Redwine, Shannon Wait, Robert Howell, Alexander Dixon, and B. Pagels-Minor. Thank you as well to everyone who spoke to me anonymously and who trusted me to share their thoughts and experiences. Without you, this book could not exist, and I am grateful to each and every one of you.

Thank you to all my friends who supported me and let me bounce thoughts and ideas off them along the way. Josh, Joseph, Jacob, Fuzzy, Alicia, Ruby, Kevin, Matt, Grace, Adam, Grace, Tim, and Sophie, you are all wonderful. Thank you for your patience with me along the way.

And finally, thank you most of all to Zach and Jeff, for being there through it all, for supporting me and believing in me. I couldn't have done any of it without you.

Resources

NLRB forms and overviews

1. https://www.nlrb.gov/resources/nlrb-process

2. https://www.nlrb.gov/sites/default/files/attachments/pages
   /node-195/501_3-21.pdf

3. https://www.nlrb.gov/sites/default/files/attachments/pages
   /node-195/nlrb_502rc_2-18.pdf

Further information about unions and organizer training

1. https://www.polygon.com/23485977/video-game-unions
   -guide-explainer

2. https://guide.unitworkers.com/

3. https://techworkerhandbook.org/

4. https://code-cwa.org/organizer-training

5. https://aflcio.org/about-us/programs/organizing-institute

6. https://education.cwu.org/

7. https://uaw.org/members/labor-lab/

Financial and infrastructure resources

1. https://home.coworker.org/projects/coworker-solidarity-fund/

2. https://guide.unitworkers.com/

Whistleblower support

1. https://thesignalsnetwork.org/

2. https://www.nlrb.gov/about-nlrb/who-we-are/regional-offices

Other excellent books

1. There is Power in a Union: The Epic History of Labor in America – Phillip Dray

2. Labor Law for the Rank & Filer: Building Solidarity While Staying Clear of the Law – Staughton Lynd and Daniel Gross

3. Secrets of a Successful Organizer – Alexandra Bradbury, Jane

Slaughter, and Mark D. Brenner

4. Organizing for Social Change : A Manual for Activists - Kim Bobo, Jackie Kendall, Steve Max

About the Author

Janneke Parrish is a tech activist and one of the founders of the tech union, AppleTogether. In 2021, her work at Apple made headlines around the world, and her case continues to impact the course of American labor law.

When not upending power structures, Parrish enjoys mountaineering, rock climbing, and writing. She lives in Amsterdam with her partner, Zach. *The Tech Worker's Guide to Unions* is her first book.

You can visit Parrish online at www.jannekeparrish.com

www.ingramcontent.com/pod-product-compliance
Lightning Source LLC
LaVergne TN
LVHW010818200726
843507LV00003B/631